SWAN

SWAN

An Hachette UK Company
www.hachette.co.uk
Summersdale Publishers Ltd
Part of Octopus Publishing Group Limited
Carmelite House
50 Victoria Embankment
LONDON
EC4Y 0DZ
UK

www.summersdale.com

Printed and bound by CPI Group (UK) Ltd, Croydon, CR0 4YY

ISBN: 978-1-80007-336-4

Substantial discounts on bulk quantities of Summersdale books are available to corporations, professional associations and other organisations. For details contact general enquiries: telephone: +44 (0) 1243 771107 or email: enquiries@summersdale.com.

SWAN

Portrait of a Majestic Bird,
from Mythical Meanings to
the Modern Day

DAN KEEL

summersdale

CONTENTS

Preface | 7

Prologue | 9

Chapter One – The Mute Swan | 15

Chapter Two – The Lover | 49

Chapter Three – The Fighter | 85

Chapter Four – The Myth | 123

Chapter Five – The Aviator | 171

Chapter Six – The Inspiration | 193

Chapter Seven – The Future | 215

Epilogue | 227

Timeline | 231

Essential Swan Facts and Stats | 234

Want to Know More About Swans? | 237

List of Illustrations | 243

About the Author | 245

Acknowledgements | 246

Notes | 247

Select Bibliography | 250

Index | 252

PREFACE

The swan is a creature with two natures: both a lover and a fighter, a graceful angel and a clumsy oaf; both an inspiration behind the design of some of our most beautiful aircraft and a natural hazard responsible on occasions for bringing them down. This book explores these contrasts while studying the swan's life and death via courtship, mating, feeding, predation and, in some cases, migration. We'll also shed light on its relationship with humans and examine some of the myths and legends surrounding one of our largest and strongest birds. Can a swan really break your arm? Does swan meat really taste like fishy mutton? Can you be locked up for killing a swan? Woven into all of the above are my observations and experiences of this most magnificent of creatures over three decades of birdwatching and many years of freelance nature journalism and wildlife photography.

But when I say 'swan', what do I mean? After all, Britain is lucky enough to have three different species: the mute swan, the Bewick's swan and the whooper swan. I will be focusing on the mute swan throughout this book – that's the one with the orange beak. Unless stated otherwise, when I speak of 'swans' I'm talking about mutes, and unless you are a birdwatcher this is probably the only species you've ever seen. Unlike Bewick's and whooper swans, which are shy, easily spooked and pretty hard to track down, mute swans are generally tame, trusting of humans and plentiful in the lakes and rivers near our homes.

It is probably the mute swan's relative ease around human beings which has allowed me to spend hundreds of hours observing and photographing them in our waterways, our meadows and even up among the clouds (I also happen to be a qualified pilot). Yes, their beauty fascinates me, but so does their disposition, their aura and their history.

Swans were swimming in our rivers and waddling in our wetlands long before humans arrived. As a species, they have seen so much and overcome so many challenges. They possess an adaptability and a resolve which over the years I have spent many hours exploring. More recently, I have also become obsessed with giving them a voice. You see, unlike most birds, mute swans really are mute. They can't sing like a robin. They can't even call like a crow. A hiss or an occasional grunt is all they can muster. It's important we speak out on their behalf. So thank you for joining me in singing this song for the mute swan.

PROLOGUE

Winter birdwatching is the most rewarding kind. The cold light of the New Year brings a clarity of image absent in the warm, hazy summer months. If you are lucky enough to rise to a clear blue sky, the prize can be enormous. With fewer leaves on the trees and humans to alarm, the chances of catching a glimpse of nature's wildlife are improved. The backdrop – an icy lake, a frost-coated tree or a snow-smothered knoll – enhances the shot. But a 'shot' does not require a lens. Many a memory remains beautiful when we live in the scene, rather than striving for a perfect picture of it.

It is on one such frosty January morning, without a camera, that I push my way up a small mound towards my favourite tree in the world. The satisfying crunch of fresh frost under my boots is briefly interrupted by the oak's giant roots and a pothole obscured by the packed snow. Eyes front or skywards, scanning for movement in the trees and oblivious to what lies beneath their feet, a birder can easily turn an ankle on a day like this. But, as I regain my balance, I'm reminded that snow and frost bring far greater threats to Britain's favourite bird than balance of body. For this red-breasted member of the thrush family, such conditions can tip the scales of life in favour of death.

Robins are rarely killed by the cold alone, but instead perish from the starvation that follows. The male hops and skips between fallen twigs, stabbing his short, thin, black beak into the snow, desperately searching for insects, seeds and worms. Far from plump, his breast is waning, flat and bedraggled. A week of sub-zero temperatures is taking its toll. He pokes and prods his way through an inch of snow only to find a thick layer of frost sheltered from the weak winter sun. Today is the tenth day of Christmas (3 January). What for humans is a festive scene is instead a bitter fight for survival for the robin. When seeds and fruit are scarce, the bird relies heavily on ground-dwelling prey such as spiders, snails, worms, caterpillars and other grubs. Unlike blue tits and great tits, he rarely feeds in trees, instead foraging on the ground. But the ground can no longer be found, buried under an inch of snow and hard frost.

The arrival of a dunnock complicates his plight further still. Similar in size but far less fearsome than his songbird cousin, this male is in better condition. Plump and with a shiny finish, he hops to within a yard of the great oak's base. The battle is a short-lived affair. The robin is pound-for-pound one of the UK's most violent birds, a fiercely territorial lone wolf. With a short, sharp beat of his wings, he lurches at the invader in a jerky stabbing motion. The strike is three-pronged. Two feet and a bill come crashing down upon the dunnock, which swiftly retreats to the safety of a dense holly bush.

But why is the red-breast so viciously defending this seemingly barren tree-base? Suddenly all becomes clear. The heavens open to reveal a shower of brown, greasy dust raining down upon the snow. Just eight feet above the ground, among the sturdy branches of the mighty arms of an oak, a second story is unfolding – one which could yet help the robin survive the day. Swinging gently in the cold breeze is a cluster of six suet-balls, or 'fat balls' – man-made tennis-ball-sized spheres of nutrition packed full of seeds and beef suet, held together with lard. They have triggered quite a commotion. It is here that bird-table politics play out in full view. A great spotted woodpecker, the king of the garden, perches proudly above the trove, leaning down to dismantle one of the swinging balls with its thick, grey beak.

Woodpeckers are messy eaters. Food pours down towards the snow on which the robin stands. The robin cocks his head, jabs at the edible scraps and swallows while scanning the horizon for threats. He disappears into the foliage for ten seconds and then returns, repeating the ritual while the woodpecker continues its feeding frenzy.

Two minutes pass before the greedy woodpecker disappears into the woodland with a short, sharp 'keek' call. It takes less than a minute for the pecking-order's next-in-line to appear on the scene: a pair of great tits, clinging to the feed ball's string, never daring more than three bites before disappearing into the labyrinth of branches. Then come the smaller blue tits, squeaking like mice, sometimes mixing with their great tit relatives but mostly waiting for a short moment to feed alone. Then finally the tiny coal tits. Appearing from a neighbouring pine tree, they have been watching the drama unfold, biding their time for even the shortest of windows to pick-pocket their share. Once the larger birds have had their fill, they take their chance – but tentatively. My heart melts at their nervous, frenetic behaviour – landing, scanning for predators, one tiny peck, scanning for predators, fleeing to the ferns, scanning for predators, eating, scanning for predators. What a life! Forever in fear of being snatched and gobbled up by a passing sparrowhawk.

As I watch the coal tits make the most of this narrow opportunity, my eyes are drawn to another minuscule ball of feathers hopping between the oak and the fern. Never straying from the weakest and slimmest of branches, the goldcrest feels safer flitting around the edges of the oak, away from the bigger, bolder birds which might do it harm. This female will not join the feast, though she may dare to forage for scraps once the robin has left. But the faint 'sree-sree-sree' of Britain's smallest bird is being drowned out by something else. Something's wrong. She disappears and my eyes return to the tree's base. Nothing – no robin and no more falling food. Just the fat balls gently swaying in the breeze.

Next, a moving broken shadow and the soft but growing sound so familiar to my childhood – a rhythmic 'wou-wou' of beating wings. The perfect V-formation of five begins to break as it skims the tops of the trees. Oblivious to the feast they have ruined, these splendid white beasts descend with slow, regular beats towards the partly frozen lake just a few hundred yards from where I stand. From the top of the knoll, the winter sun behind me, I have a perfect view of one of nature's great spectacles.

Swans in flight are truly majestic. The huge webbed feet tucked neatly out of sight behind the tail feathers give the bird a slick, sleek shape in which feet, tail, torso and neck form one natural horizontal line with the head dipped ever so slightly in front.

Only the lake's centre section has thawed. As the leader approaches, the wings fall silent as he glides above the water, three feet high. The nose which has been dipped, begins to rise in the landing flare; the body so perfectly horizontal when passing the oak, now diagonal with the nose pointing skywards. As every beginner pilot knows, the last few seconds of a good landing leave you blind to the ground, with only the sky, the clouds or the darkness of night in your sights. A metre above the water and the male at last lowers the undercarriage. Two short legs protrude as he gently beats his wings to cushion the return to earth. From a distance of 300 yards I hear both feet skim the water's surface, high but descending in pitch as the legs are plunged deeper into the black icy darkness.

The remainder of the flight is far less graceful. Missing the small area of rippled water, the remaining four touch down on snow-peppered ice. Accustomed to the rough grip of grass or the soft cushion of water, they slip on the icy glass and tumble onto their sides sending mallards and pochards rushing to the sky. Rising quickly but sheepishly, the four clumsy stragglers – a mixture of males and females – now display their least elegant trait: walking or, more correctly, waddling back to their friend in the water. As they do, I scan the edges of the lake. One fox, three greylag geese, four dogs and six humans have all stopped to watch the show, oblivious to anything else.

The swan is a scene-stealer, a show-stopper of the highest order, inspiring Greek tragedies, poems, ballets, songs, art, boats and aircraft. The eminent eighteenth-century naturalist Georges-Louis Leclerc, Comte de Buffon, could not have put it better when he wrote this of the swan: 'displaying a thousand graceful attitudes... there is not a more beautiful figure in all of nature.'

Chapter One

THE
MUTE
SWAN

The swan is a complex character, bursting with contradiction. Only a handful of this planet's birds remain loyal to their partner for life; even fewer have a propensity for the kind of violence required to drown your dog. Its graceful majesty in flight and on water has inspired some of our greatest architecture, dance, paintings and literature. Yet its awkward dawdling on land has provoked little beyond ridicule and slapstick comedy.

More than 10,000 bird species exist across the world. To date, I have seen 214 of them in the UK and 600 across the planet. Not one has come close to matching the swan for drama and grace, affection and ferocity. And not one has ever displayed all four traits in a single minute like a swan can in springtime.

We will soon explore these contrasts by getting underneath the feathers of the mute swan. But it would be rude not to give a brief shout out to Britain's two other species. After all, one day you might find yourself staring at a yellow-billed swan rather than an orange one, and wouldn't it be nice to know what it is?

The Bewick's and whooper swans (with a silent 'w') are both beautiful and fascinating birds which without doubt are worthy of books of their own. The Bewick's is the smallest of our swans. It has a yellow and black bill (or 'beak', depending on your preference), is less stocky than a whooper and considerably shorter than a mute. In recent years it has made a name for itself by marking the beginning of the Great British wintertime. Arriving from deepest darkest Arctic Russia, hundreds of Bewick's swans descend on Slimbridge Wetland Centre on the River Severn in Gloucestershire, to be closely followed by chilly weather.

Researchers have recorded the arrival of the year's first Bewick's swan at the centre every year since 1963. In 2018, one of the latest 'first arrivers', a bird called Trotsky, touched down on 10 November. It was later than usual, as the autumn months had been mild. Sure enough, frosty weather soon followed. Unsurprisingly this research is not conducted with weather forecasting in mind but with conservation. Sadly, the news is not good. Populations are declining, with a wider study suggesting numbers of Bewick's migrating to northern Europe have plummeted from 29,000 just 50 years ago to 18,000 in 2010. Illegal hunting and loss of habitat in Russia could be to blame.

Some ornithologists refuse to label the Bewick's an individual species separate from North America's whistling swan. Many bird geeks continue to argue that both are mere sub-groups of a species more generally known as the tundra swan. If you care to look into the issue, you'll find the Bewick's to have much more yellow in its bill than the whistling swan – but a different appearance does not necessarily mean a different species.

When it comes to the whooper swan, there is no doubting its validity as a species. The UK's third swan, the whooper is faring slightly better, although it is still in decline.

It migrates to the UK from northern Europe in wintertime and is once again distinguished from the Bewick's by its bill (the whooper's yellow section tapers off into a black tip) and, more easily, by its tremendous 'whooping' call, which is often compared to an old-fashioned car horn.

Both the Bewick's and the whooper are undoubtedly beautiful birds. In fact, most birdwatchers would find themselves far more excited at the sight of a Bewick's or the honk of whooper than they would the glimpse or the hiss of a mute. But say the word 'swan' and for most British people it's the orange-billed mute swan they think of, a much-loved bird that brings so much joy to a relaxing walk by a lake or river. How do I know? Well, the stats don't lie. In 2015 the ornithologist David Lindo (also known as the Urban Birder) unveiled the results of a nationwide poll designed to find Britain's favourite species and nominate a national bird. From more than 200,000 votes cast, the robin was the emphatic winner with 34 per cent of the total. The barn owl followed with 12 per cent, and the mute swan finished 7th with a six per cent share behind the blackbird, wren, red kite and kingfisher. The top 10 was completed by the blue tit, hen harrier and puffin. The Bewick's and whooper swans did not get a mention.*

---

* At the time of writing, the robin has not yet secured *official* status as the UK's national bird.

Britain's favourite bird:

Robin	34%	(75,623 votes)
Barn Owl	12%	(26,191)
Blackbird	11%	(25,369)
Wren	9%	(19,609)
Red Kite	6%	(14,057)
Kingfisher	6%	(13,922)
Mute Swan	**6%**	**(13,480)**
Blue Tit	6%	(13,123)
Hen Harrier	5%	(12,390)
Puffin	5%	(10,674)

You may notice that garden birds fared well compared to other groups. This makes perfect sense given it was a public poll, not a vote among birdwatchers. In fact, some 60 per cent of voters were not associated with birdwatching or conservation organisations in any shape or form. Birdwatchers, you see, are naturally exposed to a far wider range of species and often fall in love with a particular bird following a specific trip. I, for example, have had a particular penchant for hoopoes, with their bright orange plumage and crest, ever since the time I spent a week's worth of lunch breaks scouring a nearby industrial estate in Reading for this lovely bird after it was spotted by a team of local builders. A birdwatcher is more than happy to sit for six hours in the confines of a freezing bird hide on Sheppey's windswept estuary for a glimpse of a lesser white-fronted goose. But it's fair to surmise that most folk feel closest to the birds that visit them in the comfort of their back garden.

It is worth noting that while Britain is a country of gardens and gardeners, this passion is less common in parts of Europe. I once proudly described my garden to a Spanish colleague, detailing my bird table, daffodils, narrow stone path and hand-built shed. I pondered aloud the feasibility of a vegetable patch in a city garden and whether a picket fence made from truck pallets would afford my carrots adequate protection. By the time I had looked up from my backyard daydream, she had walked off – a mixture of confusion and utter boredom.

But unless you live on a lake, a river or a farm, the chances of meeting a swan over a cup of tea in your garden are somewhat slim. So, what makes the swan popular enough to make the top 10? And what prevents it from beating the robin?

We've already discussed the great access we have to swans compared with other birds. They are often quite tame, view humans as a source of food, and nest in places which are easy to spot. I can think of few British birds whose nesting and brooding of chicks can be so easily watched, studied and enjoyed. Perhaps only the coot and the moorhen come close. In short, we can interact with a swan and enjoy its quirks in a way that isn't possible with most other species.

Maybe we Brits see something of ourselves in the swan. It is calm and composed on top, a portrait of stoicism and tranquillity, but this disguises a relentless and tiring pedal underneath.

The robin, however, has one distinct advantage – it is found just about everywhere. Voters the length and breadth of the country will see robins near their own homes. They'll hear them too. Many birds sing only when defending nesting territory or attracting mates. Robins are different, defending feeding territories with their explosive song throughout the year. Cities, towns, villages, seaside resorts, woodlands both deciduous and coniferous, shrubland, heathland and mountains are all suitable for robins; the same cannot be said for swans.

Then there's the swan's notorious temper. While the swan is undoubtedly an icon of love, romance, peace and grace, very few people will have been hissed at or attacked by a robin. In fact, most would describe the robin as friendly despite its propensity for violence against other birds. A swan, while sometimes friendly, won't sit on your spade while you're watering the plants or digging up weeds in the place you call home.

Maybe the mute swan suffers from being the 'almost champion'. After all, it's not the UK's biggest bird – that title belongs to the whooper swan. It's not even the heaviest flying bird in the world – the kori bustard has that one sewn up.[1] But while records and titles may be important to some people, they aren't to me. Enjoying birds is an art not a science. I will never fully understand why some birds are more popular than others. But I can take a stab at explaining why the swan is and always will be number one for me. To get there, I must begin by asking an even more important question – why birds at all?

Growing up with swans

Birdwatching is one of the world's fastest-growing hobbies. In 2017 the luxury travel magazine *Condé Nast Traveller* described birding as the year's 'unlikeliest craze'. The 2008 financial meltdown, the recession and the economic troubles which followed encouraged people to seek cheaper pastimes. Many who were no longer able to afford sailing, ballroom dancing or whatever expensive hobby they had enjoyed in better times, turned instead to activities that were completely free. Countryside hikes, weekend bike rides and Sunday morning strolls became increasingly popular. We began to notice more about our surroundings: the change in the trees, the depth of the rivers and, of course, the wildlife near our homes.

Next we faced a new challenge, a global pandemic, which saw us confined to our neighbourhoods for long stretches of time during what turned out to be one of the sunniest springs and most glorious summers in living memory. And what did we do? We explored the world around us, the one we usually fail to notice. And having caught the bug, as lockdown eased but travel abroad was still almost impossible, we looked further afield in our own country, started noticing the subtle changes to our natural surroundings that are part of the seasonal rhythm to which in normal times we pay almost no heed.

Covid also made us more conscious of our mental health. We questioned the need and even the wisdom of the daily commute. We began to appreciate the incredible potential of nature to help free our minds, stimulate our creativity and live a more peaceful life.

But again, I hear you ask, why birds? Why not fish or mammals?

First and foremost, there are lots of birds to be seen. There are of course plenty of mammals too – but how often do we really spot them on our walks? Deer? Yes, if you live in the right area. Foxes and squirrels? Absolutely, in both towns and countryside. But I often go weeks without seeing a rat, a mouse, a vole, a shrew or even a rabbit. I could go months without seeing a stoat, years without seeing a hedgehog and decades without seeing a badger.

But birds are everywhere. While it's true that many species are in steep decline, they are still abundant – in our skies, our trees, our waterways, our fields and on the roofs of our homes. We can hear them too. I defy anyone to walk around London without hearing a feral pigeon, a blackbird or a herring gull. For those who decide to take spotting birds more seriously, there are more than enough species to keep things interesting. In contrast there are only 100 mammal species in the UK, and many people only see between 10 and 30 in their lifetimes because a large proportion are rare dolphins, whales and bats. But there is one reason to enjoy watching birds which for me supersedes all others: they fly.

I dare not speak on behalf of mankind but I suggest most humans have at some time wished they could simply take off and fly away. Think of the times you've spent sitting in traffic or standing on crowded trains, desperate to return home to enjoy the evening. Or the daydreams spent yearning to fly away to warmer climes without the expense, the security checks and the transfers. Above all, think of the time you've spent feeling physically and mentally trapped, desperate to rise above the claustrophobic rat race for the liberty and infinity of flight. Every path we tread eventually narrows, the buildings close in or the road comes to an end. But not the sky. The sky is infinite.

Our love of flight is evident in so many walks of life. Our favourite football goals see the ball fly into the top corner, the goalkeeper briefly levitating – arms outstretched, feet off the ground – as he reaches out in vain. In cricket there is no more exhilarating sight than a sweep stroke which launches the ball high over the boundary for six.

Humans have been working to design the smoothest, fastest, most manoeuvrable flying machines for more than a century. Jet packs and levitation devices could one day become the norm, and for those without the skills to create one (or the money to buy one), there is a plentiful supply of activities to mimic the sensation. Extreme activities such as sky-diving, wing-suit flying and even bungee-jumping are perhaps popular not only for the adrenaline rush, but because they bring us closer than ever to the world as seen through the eyes and felt through the wings of a bird.

But birds make flight infinitely more fun. They fly fast, they fly slow, they hunt in the air, they fire themselves skyward and dive down to land. Some, like the kestrel, can hover. Some, like the hummingbird, can fly backwards. Others, like the swift, can even sleep on the wing. Birds do all of these things more beautifully and more effortlessly than anything we will ever build ourselves.

The excitement and freedom expressed in flight is something which captured my imagination from the day I was old enough to stand on two feet and stare at the sky. But there was also some gentle encouragement from a dad who became a birdwatcher after exploring the meadows of Hampshire and Berkshire with his father. My dad is the best birdwatcher I know – and I do mean birdwatcher, not ornithologist and not twitcher. Ornithologists are scientists. Dissatisfied with strolling the hills and woodlands near their homes, they study the behaviour and movements of birds in forensic detail, often focusing on a particular trait of a single species. Twitchers on the other hand are the extreme sport athletes of birdwatching. They travel the length and breadth of the country and sometimes the world, in search of particular birds. Their species totals are impressive and their dedication unimpeachable. But twitching is too stressful for birdwatchers. In fact, believe it or not, the very name 'twitcher' is said to derive from the facial twitching that some enthusiasts exhibit when getting anxious at the thought of missing a rare bird.

And so, if like me you enjoy watching birds, hate stress and have little interest in dissecting the diet of a great grey shrike or studying the tail bobbing of a lapwing, you are probably a birdwatcher. My dad is a birdwatcher. He knows a lot about birds but particularly those in west Berkshire. His joy and satisfaction derive not from the ticking of birds from a list nor the thrill of a chase, but from observing what turns up in his local patch.

He could tell you when he first saw a Berkshire swallow for any given year. (In 2015 it was 10 April. In 2020 it was 8 April.) He could tell you how many different types of birds he has seen from his living-room window (82, since you ask). His lifetime number of species currently stands at 266. Of those, he's seen 221 of them in his home county. He keeps diaries, lists, and lists of lists. But his contentment is rooted in the love of birds not in the pursuit of birds. Indeed, as the years roll on, he takes more satisfaction from watching the same birds in his back garden than from the search for new ones farther afield. He taught me how to enjoy watching common birds rather than bemoaning the lack of rare ones. He taught me to check the edges of lakes for waders and the tops of pylons for kestrels. But most importantly, he taught me the songs.

Knowing your patch's common sights, sounds and songs inside out gives you a huge advantage over other birdwatchers. Accustomed to seeing redshank and wigeon ducks on Theale's gravel-pit lake, my dad's interest is piqued whenever that lake is deserted. He instinctively knows to scour the hedgerows, fenceposts and skies for a predator. Sometimes he will find a peregrine stalking beneath the looming grey clouds. Sometimes he won't. But the point is that without that local knowledge, an outsider would have seen just an empty lake, given up and moved onto the next. Dad sees not an empty lake, but a scene gone awry – a potential hunt.

Birdsongs and calls give birdwatchers a similar grounding. My number one tip to birdwatchers is 'Keep your head up, not down.' My second is 'Learn ten songs.' Only when I made a concerted effort to learn the calls of some of Britain's most common birds did my birdwatching and identification really improve. Here are my ten:*

---

* I have excluded the obvious birds like cuckoo ('cook-ooh'), tawny owl ('twit-twoo') and mallard duck ('quack').

1. Blackbird
2. Robin
3. House sparrow
4. Blue tit
5. Great tit
6. Wood pigeon
7. Collared dove
8. Wren
9. Song thrush
10. Coal tit

The results were instant. Every time I heard a bird that was not on this list, I knew it could be something rare. Just a week after learning the call of a collared dove I heard a similar but different call from a medium-sized oak tree near home. Rather than the familiar 'coo-coo-cuk' of a collared dove, I heard a slightly deeper 'ooo-woo, ooo-woo'. Upon closer inspection with binoculars it became clear this was in fact a stock dove. Without the knowledge of the unusual call, I would not have bothered looking in the tree. The eternal presence of birds in my eyes and ears, the exhilaration of watching them fly, and the gentle encouragement from a loving dad meant I was hooked. I had become a birdwatcher. But why mute swans? Why not kingfishers or kestrels?

My own friendship with swans began in childhood, watching them cruise effortlessly overhead before floating gently down onto lakes and rivers with a satisfying, refreshing skim and a splash. I have always been fascinated with flight. I love watching all birds take to the skies. But there is no other species which matches the swan for drama on take-off and landing. The touchdowns were a spectacle I became obsessed with in my early birding years. I observed how the slick contours of the body and neck were perfectly maintained until only a few feet above the water. Then, and only then, was the undercarriage lowered. It was as if these proud, majestic beings were determined to maintain their unblemished beauty for as long as possible, reluctant to reveal their two enormous ugly feet until absolutely necessary (see picture 7). I loved how their wings ceased to beat as the feet eased down. Instead, they soared like a buzzard for a brief moment before gently flicking their wings a mere six or seven beats and caressing the plane of the water.

But there was also a connection with swans which was frustratingly absent with other birds. The English author J. A. Baker, who wrote a book about peregrine falcons, once described birdwatching as walking 'within a hoop of red-hot iron, a hundred yards across, that sears away all life'. This was how I felt as a child. No matter how quiet my footsteps, nor how noble my intentions, every living animal seemed terrified of my presence – but not the swan.

Swans were my companions, glad to join me for a lakeside lunch, content to share my dining space and, on occasion, brave enough to eat from my hand. Like any true friend they were also reliable. One summer my brothers and I took pleasure in predicting their departure and arrival times at Thatcham Lakes. The same young pair would launch themselves into the skies in search of grazing lands at around 8.15 a.m. and return to roost at 7.45 p.m. Over ten days their departure and arrival times fell within the same 20-minute window – more punctual than any airline I know.

But it was their loyalty which also drew me in. Coupled swans are noted for their dedication to one another, but I also found them loyal to me. They recognised me, trusted me and would choose to head *my* way, not the way of rival children. It is easy to take for granted our fortune at having such elegant birds on these British Isles, both comparatively common and eager to share a good relationship with humans despite our repeated betrayal of their trust (something we'll explore later). Even swans I have encountered which are not so tame are open to being approached, once tempted with a suitable treat. In short, I had a bond with swans which I could not forge with any other bird. But it was in 2005, two years after passing my flying exams, that my friendship with the mute swan blossomed into a love affair.

Flying with swans

Visibility over the North Wessex Downs is good, but a light haze obscures parts of the Isle of Wight more than 40 miles away. I have spent the last hour flying at 2000 feet, searching for chalk white horses etched into the Wiltshire hills west of Marlborough. Eight of these figures can be seen around the county. Some are 250 years old and 180 feet wide. Nobody really knows who designed these fantastic works, or why. Some people suggest they are a somewhat belated celebration of King Alfred's victory at the Battle of Ethandun in 878.

After snapping a few blurred shots from the cockpit, I turn to fly home with a stiff breeze on my tail. The beauty of flying a Cessna 150 lies in the wings-on-top design giving me an undisturbed view of the land below. On this warm sunny May afternoon, I have spotted red kites and buzzards from above. I would never suggest I was 'seeing the world through their eyes'. For one thing, I can't sharply focus on prey a mile away like they can. Neither can my eyes detect the ultraviolet light emitted from the urine trails of animals (many raptors, such as kestrels, follow the urine trails of prey, leading them to their dinner). But I do get a tranquil perspective that's absent among the hustle and bustle of flightless folk like me.

This urge to float above the world for a true sense of my surroundings has been with me since I first watched swans propel themselves into the skies above Thatcham.

Swan watching, however, was not enough to satisfy my obsession with flight. Aged 10, I broadened out into plane spotting with regular trips to aircraft museums and air shows. I began saving every penny I could in the hope of one day learning how to fly. It took eight years to save the cash to travel to South Africa for intensive flight training. Five weeks later and I was a fully qualified private pilot, free to use my licence in small planes in the UK. It is the best decision I ever made.

On this particular day, I am returning home to Popham Airfield, a quaint flying club sandwiched between the North Wessex Downs to the north and the Sussex Downs to the south. The aircraft I am flying is named G-AN (Golf, Alpha, November). To my left is the Hampshire town of Basingstoke. Far beyond that towards the horizon I can just make out London and the blinking light atop Canary Wharf's One Canada Square. Above the aircraft's nose to the south I can see Popham's two grass landing strips surrounded by wheat fields and acre upon acre of rapeseed crops.

Today's approach and landing require a steady descent, taking in some of the area's best natural views. It was during this slow descent towards the ground that the airfield's radio operator tried and failed to speak to me:

> Radio operator: 'Golf-Alpha-November,
> report final'

In English: *Please call me when you're on your final approach to land. If I don't hear from you, I will assume you are either in great trouble or dead.*

At this point I was supposed to acknowledge receipt and repeat back the words: 'Report final, Golf-Alpha-November'.

Radio operator: 'Golf-Alpha-November, report… final'

As I stared, open-mouthed through my right window I was completely oblivious to the increasingly irate operator in my headphones.

Radio operator: 'Golf…….. Alpha……… November……… report……………….. final'

I've always hated clichés and remember all too well the rollickings I received from newspaper editors after including quotes from people in my stories who said they were 'speechless', especially when they then proceeded to talk at length. There are few moments in life when I have been overcome with emotion to the point of being rendered mute – a close encounter with a snake in Turkey springs to mind. But that's exactly what I was as I cruised past a pair of similarly named swans at exactly 800 feet.

Swans tend to cruise at around 40 mph, compared to my Cessna's 90 mph, meaning my view was brief but clear. I recall the slow regularity of the wingbeats, the faint rusty orange on the heads, the large dark feet swept underneath and the dark, rich orange of the bill.

At such close range, I could make out the individual wing feathers, the underwings' darker shade and the neat points to the tails. I remember staring at their long elegant necks, marvelling at the strength required to keep them level when the full force of gravity was urging them to droop. I recall the shallow U-shaped arch of the wing on the down stroke and the splayed wingtip feathers appearing to flick the birds forward. I remember for that one moment feeling completely and utterly carefree – a frightening thought given where I was.

Who knows what was going through their minds as a noisy monstrosity of a machine trundled alongside. They did not divert course nor height and showed not a hint of distress. But most incredible was their nonchalant dismissal of the light summer breeze. As I pulled up beside them, a nasty gust blew me towards them from left to right. I was forced to fight the controls with my arms and feet to maintain my course, swinging left and right in the air. But not the swans; the slightest of wing tilts was all these superior flyers needed to stay on track – their myriad muscles and feathers working in tandem to steady their course. How amazing it would have been to slow down my machine to a crawl and fly beside them for just a few moments more, but such low speeds are dangerous in a Cessna. To my delight, as I finally tore my gaze away from them and pushed the aircraft down and left towards the airfield, the swans did briefly alter their bearings – following my curve across to the runway for just a few brief moments, before continuing their voyage.

But where were they going? Why were they going there? Was this the beginning of an epic journey? The end of a short one? Swans rarely fly above 500 feet and usually do so only when migrating, when they sometimes reach altitudes of more than 2,000 feet. So at 800 feet, the literature would suggest the end of a long flight to pastures new, though even then I knew better than to overanalyse the scene, for fear of losing the magic.

Once safely back on Earth I briefly considered a sloppy attempt to track them down. Where could they be? The nearby golf course perhaps? A lake, three miles away? A supermarket car park? But why ruin the perfect memory? Imagine if I had discovered the pair waddling towards a crowd of people in search of bread – what a shame that would have been! The moment must not be disturbed.

There are three things I learned from this flight. The first is that Wiltshire's white horses look better from the ground than from the air. Unless you are a stunt pilot happy to buzz angry residents with *Top Gun*-style low-level flybys, chalk horses are not big enough to warrant a trip to the skies.

The second is that, at that stage in my flying career, I could be safely described as 'a below-average' pilot. This does not mean I was a poor pilot, nor necessarily unsafe. For every activity, there is always an average level of competence, meaning there are always those 'above' and those 'below' the mean. But having been rendered deaf, dumb and immobile at the sight of two flying animals, I clearly had some work to do.

The third thing I learned is that the visual form of a swan is near-enough perfect in every conceivable way. In this magical moment I had seen the mute swan at its most sublime.

The Comte de Buffon, who wrote 36 volumes of his *Histoire Naturelle*, knew a thing or two about nature's beauty. He was spot-on when he declared:

> *In its form, we find no broken or harsh lines; in its motions, nothing constrained or abrupt; but the roundest of contours, and the easiest of transitions; the eye wanders over the whole with unalloyed pleasure, and with every change of position every part assumes a new grace.*

The queen of the bird world

Flying with swans was a truly magical moment which I will likely never repeat. From that day on, I was officially a swan addict, desperate to study them up close, to photograph them and to understand their character, their anatomy and their roots. What motivates a swan, what do they eat and where did they come from?

Understanding the genesis of swans can bizarrely be explained using the story of my 30th birthday. As I unwrapped the gift of a shiny new bird book from my parents, I turned to my Dad and asked: *why is the swan the first bird in the bird book?* The somewhat surprising answer lies not in the size of the bird or its name or intelligence, but in its relationship with dinosaurs.

Most bird books and field guides present species in taxonomic order. The families at the top of the list (or front of the book) are thought to have more quickly broken away from the suspected common ancestor of all birds – the theropod dinosaur family.* But how on earth can scientists determine which broke away first?

Up until the 1990s, ornithologists and biologists studying where a bird first appeared on fossil records would examine its physical features to make an educated guess.

---

* Theropods all had three toes and hollow bones. The most famous was the Tyrannosaurus, but birds are thought to have evolved from much smaller (and probably feathered) theropods known as Tetanurae.

The revolutionary introduction of DNA sequencing has shown many of these estimates to be completely wrong, since when the ordering has been amended on a regular basis as new discoveries and theories emerge – much to the annoyance of birders, who had grown used to a standard ordering of species in reference guides. Recent changes now mean some books place falcons closer to parakeets than to eagles and hawks. Confused birdwatchers will also find certain waders, such as ruffs, now placed after knots rather than before, and other waders, like stints, no longer placed with small sandpipers.

Such discoveries have had ramifications for the swan too. Up until 2002 it was not the mute swan which headed up many of our bird books but the red-throated diver.[2] In fact, at that time, divers, grebes, herons, geese and even ducks were all thought to have preceded the mighty swan. But as new DNA evidence emerged, our biggest birds stormed to the top of the charts. From a purely romantic standpoint I am delighted swans now lead the way in our bird books. It seems only right that birds so big and with so much regal association should introduce our birdlife to budding birdwatchers, perched at the top of the tree, ruling over all others – the kings and queens of the bird world.

So there you have it. Swans were one of the first, if not *the* first, birds in the UK to evolve from dinosaurs, meaning they have been swimming on Earth's waters, flying in its skies and dawdling across its varied lands for 30 million years – far longer than humankind's paltry six million.[3] In fact, it is pretty safe to assume that swans are older than the lakes on which they swim. But what do we really know for certain about one of Britain's biggest birds? How is a swan different from a goose? In short, what makes a swan, a swan?

Swans are members of the Anatidae family, meaning they are water birds, adapted for swimming and floating, and can dive or duck to shallow depths. Ducks and geese are members of the same family.

This family is then divided into 43 sections known as genera. One of these genera is named *Cygnus* (Latin for swan). This genus is then divided into six species (or seven if you believe that Bewick's swans and whistling swans are different). Each has its own Latin name.

The six (seven) species are:

- mute swan – *Cygnus olor*
- whooper swan – *Cygnus cygnus*
- black swan – *Cygnus atratus*
- black-necked swan – *Cygnus melancoryphus*
- trumpeter swan – *Cygnus buccinator*
- tundra swan (Bewick's and whistling) – *Cygnus columbianus*

It is important to note that the six (or seven) species listed are the surviving swans. There are thought to be many species which once roamed the planet but which are now sadly extinct.

There is also a bird found in South America, known as a coscoroba swan. But it is widely considered to, well, not be a swan after all. Scientists could not decide what to do with it, so threw the poor coscoroba swan into its own special genus, creatively entitled *Coscoroba*. Rows over whether this bird is in fact a goose have been raging for decades. But for now the coscoroba swan is grouped in a similar way to the bearded tit, which is also known as the bearded reedling or bearded parrotbill; it is neither a tit nor a parrotbill, but has been assigned to its own family.

While today there is no doubt about the authenticity of the mute as a species, this has not always been the case. For some time it was thought the mute swans which graced our waters were different from those found in Poland near the Baltic Sea. The birds were briefly categorised separately by some as 'Royal' and 'Polish' swans due to the latter having a lighter bill and greyish-pink feet rather than black ones.[4] Scientists later agreed they were merely different subgroups of the same species.

But this still fails to explain what makes a swan a swan? Why is a mute a swan, yet a coscoroba is not? I spoke to Professor Chris Perrins at Oxford University's Edward Grey Institute of Field Ornithology. He also happens to be the Queen's swan warden, meaning he is on hand to offer biological advice about swans around the UK when and where needed. Historically, this position was called the swan master. This person was largely a figurehead who helped prevent too much stealing of other people's cygnets; technically, owners could only mark cygnets in the presence of the swan master or his deputy. That changed in 1993 when the role was divided into two – the swan marker and the swan warden. Today the swan marker performs a similar role to the previous swan master. The swan warden offers more general advice around swan welfare.

Prof Perrins explained that there are two ways of answering questions around what is and is not a swan. The first is based purely on DNA sequencing. The six species of swan listed above have DNA profiles more similar to each other than they are to, let's say, geese or ducks or the coscoroba swan. The coscoroba swan's profile has less in common with other geese than the other geese species do with each other, hence the decision to place it in its own grouping.

Prof Perrins explained that the second approach is to get an idea of how long ago those groups of animals, in our case birds, had separated sufficiently to be considered different families or species. These studies tell us quite a lot. They confirm that swans are a uniform group which descend from one common ancestor (the theropod dinosaur), and that the coscoroba swan is a bit different from all the other swans and so must have split off from them a bit earlier, though it doesn't appear in my bird books, because it is not a British bird.

As to the question of what really defines a swan, well, according to the professor, that's a much trickier question to answer. He explained: 'Put simply, there isn't a magic key character – swans don't all have purple toenails and geese yellow ones or anything handy like that. But there are a number of anatomical and behavioural characteristics which swans tend to have and geese don't.' These are relatively larger feet, relatively longer necks and unfeathered lores (the bit between eye and bill). Swans also incubate their eggs for longer and have a longer development time from hatching to flying. Taken in the round, I think we can tell a swan from a goose.

The word 'swan' is also somewhat confusing because it derives from the Indo-European root 'swen' (to sound or sing), which is strange given the mute swan rarely makes a sound beyond the occasional snort or hiss. It is certainly the case that the Greeks believed the swan's long curving neck was ideal for producing a variety of notes. But many experts believe the name is much more likely to stem from a noisy relative such as the whooper which, as we know, sounds like an old-fashioned car horn.

While the roots of the swan's name are perhaps open to debate, its physical presence is undeniable. Mute swans are the heaviest birds in the UK. While whooper swans are usually longer, mutes are stockier and pack a powerful punch.* Mutes average 1.41 m (55.2 in.) in length and weigh around 12.2 kg (26.8 lb). Females (known as pens) are slightly smaller and lighter, weighing around 9 kg (19.6 lb). However, telling the difference between males and females before the age of four is near-on impossible. Only a very brave vet, prepared to catch them and study their genitalia, would be able to tell the difference. But once a swan is four years old, it's a different matter. Males (known as cobs) can usually be identified from the females by their larger black bumps (technically called blackberries) at the base of the bill. Another way to tell is by their thicker necks, which continue to widen in adulthood. Swans lucky enough to dodge pylons, buildings, irresponsible fishermen and myriad predators can live for around 12 years, while those cared for in domestic settings, safe from these dangers and fed a nutritious diet, have been known to live up to the age of 30. Imagine how girthy their necks would be by then!

Swans around the world

While deciphering the age and sex of swans is challenging, estimating their global population is even harder. Some

* Some ornithologists regard the white-tailed eagle, with its enormous 220 cm (87 in) wingspan, as the largest UK bird.

mute swans migrate (although not to or from the UK), which complicates the matter; after all, just because fewer swans have arrived in your country doesn't necessarily mean they are dead. Similarly, just because more have arrived in your country doesn't mean global numbers have increased. Throw in the fact that it's sometimes hard to know which mute swans are wild and which are domesticated... and you can see it all turns into a bit of a mess.

What we do know, however, is that estimates in 1992 suggested the global population of mute swans was some 500,000.[5] We also know around 350,000 of these were scattered around the countries of the former Soviet Union – with huge populations in the Volga delta near Kazakhstan's border with Russia. But there is also a sizeable population in the UK, with the RSPB putting the current number at 74,000. The vast majority of these are immature, but around 6,400 pairs are thought to be breeding.

Although most mute swans are resident, some do migrate around northern Europe and Russia. Some have even been found as far east as Primorsky Krai, near Russia's border with North Korea. Others have shown up as far south as Egypt and Libya. Russia and the UK aside, large concentrations can also be found in Germany (6,800–8,300 pairs), Denmark (4,500), Poland (4,000–4,200), The Netherlands (3,000–4,000), Ireland (2,500) and Ukraine (1,200–1,700).[6]

In the UK, the RSPB has categorised mute swans as 'amber', meaning numbers are slowly declining, the most likely reason being the loss of suitable habitat. But while you're less likely to see swans in the same vast numbers as in years gone by, it's still nice to know how to refer to them when you do. According to the charity, the correct collective noun for swans is somewhat complicated. A group of swans can be referred to as a 'bevy', 'a herd', 'a game' or 'a flight'. When flying they are 'a wedge' (probably because of the shape formed by a group of swans in flight). They can only be 'a bank' when they are on the ground.

However we choose to label them, there are few better sights in nature than a group of swans floating atop a calm lake or river. This is a rare sight, so treasure every second when you see it.

A diet fit for a swan

Swans live predominantly on a diet of weeds. These include:

- Pondweed (*Potamogeton*)
- Stoneworts (*Chara*)
- Water milfoil (*Myriophyllum*)
- Wigeon grass (*Ruppia*)

- Sea arrowgrass (*Triglochin maritima*)
- Sea plantain (*Plantago maritima*)
- Salt-marsh grass (*Puccinella maritima*)
- Eel grass (*Zostera marina*).

Swans do not dive in the same way as some ducks and grebes. Instead they duck their heads under the water and often up-end themselves completely so that all you can see is their white rump facing the sky. They have 60 vertebrae, of which 25 are in the neck, which makes it ideal for fishing out weed in hard-to-get places.

Swans can hold their breath for between 10 and 13 seconds, and the upper and lower sections of the bill are serrated, allowing them to tear plants from the bed of the lake or river. If this fails, they have three strong toes to scrape at the ground or riverbed until the weed is dislodged. Once it's in their bill, the swan's powerful jaw muscles and spiny tongue can easily break down food before swallowing it, making up for their lack of teeth.

Swans can feed in the day or at night, with taste and touch allowing them to select the correct plants even when the sun has set. To ensure they maintain a body temperature of 40.5 °C (104.9 °F), they need to eat a quarter of their own bodyweight every day – that's around 3 kg (6.5 lbs) of weeds. They will often eat more than this before the moulting season, usually in July or August, when they are flightless and therefore less able to scour for food. You see, swans instinctively know they must bulk up before the tough days ahead. Once their flight feathers begin to moult, to be replaced by new fresh healthy feathers, they will be unable to travel around. They'll gobble up all the food within reach and then go hungry for four to six weeks. It's therefore vital they stock up while the going is good.

Perhaps it's fitting that as we bring this chapter to a close, we find ourselves once again discussing the swan's dual nature. This huge splendid creature, the closest bird relative to the dinosaur, with its regal mannerisms and associations, its devastating power and propensity for naked aggression, is rendered a moulting 'sitting duck' for six weeks of the year – unable to fly or travel to find food, reduced to swimming or waddling like a chump.

Buffon was nearly always glowing in his praise for the mute swan, but even he conceded:

'When it ascends from its favourite element, its motions are awkward, and its neck is stretched forward with an air of stupidity; it has indeed, the air of being only a larger sort of goose.'

Chapter Two

THE
LOVER

Like the long elegant necks of two adoring mutes, the words 'swan' and 'love' have been intertwined since the days of Greek mythology. The swan's elegant shape and majestic posture have inspired countless romantic paintings and sculptures. Its dazzling white purity is the bedrock of many tragedies, plays and poems; the unspoiled mute the metaphor of innocence and virginity.

From Plato to Shakespeare and from *Swan Lake* to 'The Ugly Duckling' (more on those later), the swan is the fulcrum of numerous myths and love stories. Let's begin with ancient Greece, where the swan was an icon of love and beauty. The Greek goddess Aphrodite was linked with passion, beauty and pleasure. She deemed the swan to be sacred, and much of the art and literature which followed either depicts her *as* a swan or as riding one. Apollo, a son of the principal god Zeus, also declared the swan to be sacred and took the bird as one of his symbols. It is said that when Zeus lavished his children with gifts, Apollo was handed a golden chariot drawn by swans. Upon his death, Apollo turned into a swan, as did all the other gifted poets of his time.

But the swan's most famous appearance in Greek myth is surely the tale of 'Leda and the Swan'. The beautiful Leda was married to King Tyndareus of Sparta. Whenever Zeus, as king of the gods, took a fancy to a mortal woman, he tended to get what he wanted, sometimes transforming himself into an animal and raping his conquest in this disguise. He longed to make love to Leda, but she always resisted. So Zeus transformed himself into a swan to seduce her and it worked. The pair made passionate love and Leda went on to lay two eggs which hatched to produce Helen (of Troy) and Polydeuces.

W. B. Yeats retold the story in his 1923 poem 'Leda and the Swan':

> *A sudden blow: the great wings beating still*
> *Above the staggering girl, her thighs caressed*
> *By the dark webs, her nape caught in his bill,*
> *He holds her helpless breast upon his breast.*
> *How can those terrified vague fingers push*
> *The feathered glory from her loosening thighs?*
> *And how can body, laid in that white rush,*
> *But feel the strange heart beating where it lies?*
> *A shudder in the loins engenders there*
> *The broken wall, the burning roof and tower*
> *And Agamemnon dead.*
> *Being so caught up,*
> *So mastered by the brute blood of the air,*
> *Did she put on his knowledge with his power*
> *Before the indifferent beak could let her drop?*

The Romans produced art inspired by the same myth. Oil lamps, marble structures and sarcophagi dating back to the first century CE all depict the infamous scene, some more explicitly than others.

Michelangelo also depicted the scene in his 1530 masterpiece *Leda and the Swan*. Sadly now lost, the painting showed Leda sprawled across a red lounger, her arm entwined with a magnificent mute swan which is rammed between her thighs.

Around the same period, Leonardo da Vinci produced two pieces of his own based on the myth – one oil and one sketch. Since then, many artists including Correggio, Tintoretto, Johann Rottenhammer, Rubens, Delacroix, Gustave Moreau and Paul Cézanne have all depicted the myth in different ways.

The story is another curious case of contrasts and contradictions involving swans. While many people embrace the story of Leda as a tale of romance, some understandably suggest the encounter more closely resembles rape. The idea of a young woman being manipulated into having sex with someone she previously rejected is a justifiably sensitive one.

In fact Leda hit the headlines in 2012 when a Mayfair gallery exhibited a dramatic modern take on the myth. According to the *Evening Standard*, an off-duty police officer took exception as he passed the Scream gallery in Bruton Street on a double-decker bus. He alerted colleagues and two uniformed officers arrived to demand the work be removed on the grounds it depicted bestiality. As it happened, the exhibition had ended and the work was already being taken down when the police showed up. There were no official complaints from the public and the incident was not recorded as a crime.

In just about every century since the start of Greek civilisation, poets, playwrights and artists have used the swan to convey tranquillity, beauty, elegance and love.

Writers have found the swan to be a poetic bird, lending itself to romantic passages in novels as well as poems about love and lust. Edmund Spenser wrote in his 1579 poem *The Shephearde's Calender* that:

> *He, were he not with love so ill bedight,*
> *Would mount as high, and sing as soote*
> *[sweetly] as Swanne.*

In 1820 Percy Bysshe Shelley wrote of swans in his piece *My Soul Is Like an Enchanted Boat:*

> *My soul is an enchanted boat,*
> *Which, like a sleeping swan, doth float*
> *Upon the silver waves of thy sweet singing*

As recently as 1944, the novel *The Ballad and the Source* by Rosamond Lehmann described the new bride Tanya with the words, 'when she moved, it was a swan moving, and the sound she made was of stirred rushes'.

Playwrights have also centred their storylines of love around the swan, as August Strindberg did in his 1901 play *Swanwhite*. The play tells the story of an angry stepmother who has a prince locked up in a tower after he falls in love with the virgin heroine (Swanwhite) rather than her own daughter. The prince escapes the tower and drowns as he swims across the open water to return to his true love. But the power of love prevails over death. The prince awakes and is reunited with his beautiful sweetheart. Fairy tales involving love and swans can be found around the globe. In China, it is said that the tears of the first empress of the Qin dynasty made a swan lake as she was killed by the emperor for disobeying an order. The people mourned her death and prayed for her soul to return to earth. Their prayers were answered when a flock of swans fell from the sky to adorn the new tear lake.

Closer to home there is a Welsh folktale from Barry Island, dating back to the early 1800s. A Glamorgan farmer is thought to have seen a stunning swan in Whitmore Bay, which removed its own wings before changing into a beautiful woman before his eyes. After bathing in the sun, the woman replaced her wings and returned to her swan form before flying away. The next time he saw her, the farmer lay in wait and seized the swan's wings to prevent her from flying off. He forced the woman to marry him and locked her wings in a solid wooden chest. One day the farmer carelessly left open the chest, leaving the woman free to collect her wings and fly off into the sunset. The grief-stricken farmer died a few months later.

When it comes to art, it is not just painters who have created masterpieces inspired by the mute swan and its association with love. Charles H. C. Baldwyn devoted a large part of his career in the early 1900s to creating porcelain swan vases. Collectors paid huge sums of money for the pieces, which depicted mute swans against a matt blue sky. More recently, Scottish artist Agnes Miller Parker made swan wood engravings, some of which are now displayed in Scotland's National Gallery, highlighting the birds' beauty and the love that exists between them.

Modern-day links of swans with love, however, are largely based on the widely held belief that swans mate for life, as we will discuss in Chapter Four – The Myth. And, of course, for a lot of people, the swan's association with true love stems from the heart produced when two swans with their classic S-shaped necks meet head to head. Wildlife photographers around the world spend thousands of hours a year striving to capture this classic image, which adorns Valentine's Day cards, music sleeves and book covers. They also enjoy capturing the irony of the flat heart shape formed by a swan's wings when swimming in anger towards an enemy. This is something you are more likely to see in spring and summer when swans aggressively defend their territory and offspring – the head coiled back like a cobra and the wings wrapped up like two rip-curl waves.

But we're getting ahead of ourselves. To really understand the swan as a lover, we must get down to the lakes, the rivers and the streams on which it lives, and watch on as instinct drives it to find a mate.

Choosing a lover

Swans, unlike their duck and geese cousins, are very slow to mature. While ducks will often mate and nest in their first year, swans will only really begin looking for a partner at the age of three or four.* Youngsters live a nomadic lifestyle, moving from flock to flock, exploring new feeding grounds, scrapping with other young swans and continuing the long road to maturity. Once this milestone has been reached they have usually completely dropped their grey adolescent feathers in favour of the stunning white ones.

Love usually begins to blossom during the swan's fourth year. Rather like a young man scanning a bar for a potential partner, the recently matured cob cruises his favourite feeding grounds in search of a mate. When a pen takes his fancy, he swims in her direction and begins bobbing his head up and down. In many cases the female simply turns and swims away – game over. We can only

---

* It has been found that cygnets in captivity tend to breed a year earlier – almost certainly due to better supplies of food.

speculate as to what makes a cob attractive to pens. Perhaps a louder snort, a more aggressive personality, even a girthier neck. There is a suggestion that young swans choose partners with markings different from their parents to avoid unhealthy in-breeding,[1] but we cannot read their minds.

One distinct possibility, however, is that females are attracted to males with bright orange bills. The Israeli biologist Amotz Zahavi was the first to propose the idea of a 'handicap principle'. He suggested that for any male animal to look attractive to a potential mate, he must demonstrate that his impressive attribute – maybe an imposingly long tail, a thick set of antlers or a rich dark mane – has come at a price. Only by paying a price can he prove he is the hard-working, high-quality specimen who is worthy of the female's affection.

The author Adam Nicolson has written extensively about puffins and suggests that female puffins keep a beady eye out for males with bright orange feet, legs and bills. That's because the colour orange comes from pigments called carotenoids which are found in fish. The theory goes that puffins with glowing orange feet are therefore excellent hunters, who have worked extremely hard and expended a huge amount of energy to look that good. They have proven themselves capable of catching copious quantities of sand eels to feed both mother and puffling. But these carotenoids do more than merely produce a pretty colour. They also act as anti-oxidants and are thought to stimulate the immune system, suggesting orange feet equal a healthy body.[2]

So how does this apply to mute swans? Well, these same carotenoids are also found in fruit, vegetables and, unsurprisingly, water plants, weeds and algae. It's possible that a cob with a bright orange bill stands a better chance of attracting a pen as he has proven his strength is great enough to rip plants from the water bed, his neck long enough to reach them and his mind sharp enough to find them in the first place. He is therefore a suitable partner who is more than capable of supplying enough weeds for mother and children and, crucially, won't drop dead while doing it.

When a pen does like what she sees, convinced this cob is the kind to produce, rear and nurture brood after brood of healthy cygnets, she bows her head in return. This offers the chance to capture the perfect heart-shaped photograph – the classic image of devotion as the two gracefully bow their heads and curve their necks into an emblem of love (see picture 2).

This is the first hint that swans possess a greater, deeper bond than the average bird. Rather than getting down to business with mating and nest building, the pair first spend months together preening and feeding each other while exploring new feeding grounds. In short, they acquaint themselves with each other, developing a close connection.

As spring draws near, the pair begin exploring the area, sometimes flying considerable distances in search of suitable nesting territory. This chapter of their lives is all about location, location, location. Swans are most definitely not communal nesters (with the notable exception of Dorset's Abbotsbury Swannery, where swans have learned to benefit from plentiful nesting material and daily meals from humans). More generally they are hugely protective of their nesting territories, which often cover areas of more than ten acres. Scientists now believe the swan's bright white plumage is not designed to camouflage the bird against a snowy backdrop, as was once thought, but the exact opposite. The white of its feathers are instead a dazzling beacon of its presence against the dark lakes and greenery of the British countryside, persuading passing swans to steer clear of occupied sites. This helps the species space itself out across the country. In cases where two pairs do fight for the same site, it is usually the incumbent couple which emerges victorious, with the losers forced to find an alternative neighbourhood.

The location of this neighbourhood is of paramount importance. It must be defendable against predators, as well as being an ample distance from other breeding swans. It also needs to offer a good supply of food and nesting material in the immediate vicinity. Once a general area has been agreed, the pair settle down for some mutual feeding and preening, ensuring they are well fed and feeling strong. Rest and conditioning are crucial if the pair is to survive the testing months ahead. Their first tiring joint enterprise is to build a home.

Building a nest

Nest building is a complex affair requiring the strongest of teamwork. The time the pair have spent becoming acquainted over the preceding weeks will now pay dividends as they embark upon the gargantuan task of building a crib for their future offspring.

Once the pair are suitably fed, preened and acquainted, the cob begins suggesting exactly where in their chosen site they should build a nest, though the female has the final say. Some hardworking and patient males have been known to suggest three or four spots by throwing nesting material in each potential spot, before their partner finally gives the nod of approval to the one she likes.

The following criteria must be met before she is satisfied:

a) Near or on one of the following:
   i) A river
   ii) A lake
   iii) Marshland
   iv) A gravel pit
   v) A reservoir
   vi) A sewage farm
   vii) A reedbed

b) Near a large supply of nesting material. (Unlike other birds, swans and geese do not like transporting twigs and grass too far).

c) Near shallow water so that food (weeds and plants) is nearby.

d) Suitable for building up a solid foundation. In other words:

   i) On a bank

   ii) Amongst a reedbed

   iii) On a small island

   iv) In water shallow enough to construct an island.

The nest building itself is a messy affair. I once watched a pair of mute swans build a nest over two weeks at Thatcham Nature Centre. At first the male began ripping up twigs, plants, moss and reeds before tossing them over his wing onto the chosen site under a willow tree. The pen eagerly arranged the material into crisscrosses and guided the mini tapestries into a large circle. This particular nest was built among the plants on the Kennet & Avon Canal, meaning floating leaves and other debris inadvertently helped build up the structure. As the days wore on, the scruffy construction was transformed into a huge circle, two yards wide and two feet tall. The centre featured a small depression scooped out by the pen while the long diameter was designed in the full knowledge that mum, dad and offspring would one day need to navigate the nest. Swans' nests are tall compared to other birds, meaning they offer a good lookout for predators and other unwelcome visitors, such as lonesome adult swans. This one was also at risk of flooding, so the pair continued to build up and up until it was nearly three feet high.

Once swans are content that their new home is strong, sturdy and secure, they can at last begin thinking about occupying it with their future children. Sadly for this Thatcham pair, the nest did not last long enough for that to happen. A violent storm washed away their weeks of hard work and I never saw them again. I hope they found a better home elsewhere.

A clutch of eggs

For mating pairs who enjoy better fortune, laying a clutch of eggs in springtime usually takes around two weeks. The act of laying an egg is a quick one lasting only a few seconds, the pen shuffling her feet up and down before settling down on the nest, pushing back her rump and squeezing out an egg. She does this roughly once every 36 hours. Regular egg laying requires regular mating sessions, and the courtship display performed beforehand is one of nature's great spectacles. The pair face off before dancing with mutual head-dipping – often submerging their heads and necks deep under water. Although their faces dip at different intervals they inevitably rise in unison.

They preen one another, gently splashing water over each other's back, tail and flank feathers before rubbing heads.

At this stage, the pair's torsos are usually semi-submerged, giving the impression they are sinking. As the courtship nears its end, the pen sinks lower still into the water before the cob approaches from behind and holds her neck with his bill. He then mounts her, his wings spreading across her back.

Most birds – both male and female – have what is known as a cloaca: an internal chamber that ends in an opening. Through this opening, a bird's sex organs – testes or ovaries – discharge sperm or eggs. Not the swan. The penis of a male swan is intromittent like a human's, meaning that it extends outside the body and is specialised for delivering sperm during copulation. Surprisingly, it is only ostriches, wildfowl (waterfowl – ducks, geese and swans) and a handful of other birds which proudly display their manhood on the outside. In the case of waterfowl, this ensures that sex can take place in the water.

The swan's penis is large in proportion to its body, but that is where the bragging rights end. Copulation lasts between three and five seconds and once coition is complete, the pair rear up together breast to breast in celebration, fully extending their necks with bills pointing towards the heavens. They let off a long and loud series of guttural snorts and, lowering their bills, flick their heads from side to side before preening one another.

One or two days usually pass between a passionate session of mating and the laying of an egg, and only one egg can be laid from each session. Sometimes the female begins laying these pale, unmarked ovals before the nest is fully complete.

Her eggs are among the largest in the world, exceeded in size only by those of flightless birds such as ostriches (15 cm/6 in. long) and emus (13 cm/5 in. long). The batch is small, usually around five or six, and rarely more than 10, with batches usually smaller the older the mating pair. Eggs are around 11 cm (4 in.) long, 7 cm (3 in.) wide and weigh roughly 340 g (12 oz.) – that's around six times heavier than a chicken egg. The weight of a mute swan's egg, compared to its body, is around 3.8 per cent, which is very low compared to most other birds.[3] For example, a typical robin's egg usually weighs the equivalent of 13 per cent of its bodyweight. In case you are wondering, the ostrich lays the lightest eggs relative to bodyweight, at just two per cent. The heaviest belongs to the kiwi – an impressive 20 per cent.

Moments before the swan's first egg drops, the pen adds some breast down feathers to the crest of the nest to cushion the fall. The remaining exposed skin will soon be used to incubate them. Swan feathers are such incredible insulators that, were they to remain attached to the mother's chest, her body heat would not transfer to the eggs. Removing a handful of these feathers means she can warm the eggs with her skin and stands a better chance of heating them to the target temperature of 38 °C (100.4 °F). Rotting vegetation is also added to create ample humidity for incubation (see picture 4).[4]

In the days building up to the laying of the first egg, the pen begins a feeding frenzy, piling on the weight and energy reserves before the difficult days ahead. She will soon, after all, be sitting on the nest for long periods, unable to feed, relying on her doting partner for food.

Only when all the eggs have been laid does she begin incubating, meaning at least one of the eggs sits unincubated for around two weeks. This ensures they will develop and hatch at roughly the same moment (within a 24-hour window), giving each cygnet an equal chance of survival. It is during the following 35 to 42 days before hatching begins that some of the swan's famously romantic traits are evident, when the male behaves like any modern-day human husband. Rarely straying far from the nest, which is often very visible to the predatory eyes of foxes and corvids, he keeps a wary eye out for intruders. He takes inordinate care of the soon-to-be mother, bringing her food, conditioning her feathers and taking her place on the nest so that she can feed for herself. In some cases, males have even been known to continue incubating the eggs alone if the pen is killed.

When away from the nest, the male sleeps by floating in the water or stands on one leg nearby with his head tucked into a wing. Naptime is usually around noon or early afternoon, and again at night, but this does not differ greatly from his usual routine. Days and weeks pass as the parents fend off unwelcome visitors while shielding their eggs from the cold wind and rain. The pen uses her bill as a spatula to turn the eggs, ensuring the whole oval remains warm at all times. The painstaking process of producing, warming and protecting this clutch is one that requires relentless attention. Sometimes that concentration can slip, as I once saw for myself.

I had stumbled across a large swan's nest in Richmond Park in southwest London. The warden had sealed off the area with a rickety picket fence held together with metal wire. The makeshift barrier contained several holes, granting the male access to and from the nest site. The nest was around four feet wide and made of twigs, weeds, a green surgical glove and the remnants of a plastic bag. It was built among 30 trees in a muddy area beside a medium-sized pond. I studied this nest from mid-April to mid-May.

13 April

The restless pen shuffles from side to side before coiling her neck around her left flank, gently nestling her chin among her feathered wings. There she lies undisturbed for five minutes before extending her long neck up toward the trees and letting off a short, gargled grunt.

Her head swings round a full 360 degrees like a lasso before returning to face me head-on. From my vantage point 20 feet away I make out the down feathers plucked and laid on the crest of the nest, the individual sticks and reeds making up the structure – larger ones at the bottom, thinner, more bendy twigs towards the top. She picks at wood chips within her reach, placing them in the scruffier areas of the nest. Her torso moves not an inch, instead she uses her 60 vertebrae to twist and turn at acute angles to reach the debris required to maintain her new home.

With another short honk she stretches her legs, fully extends her neck towards the heavens and spreads her wings with two short flaps. She has exposed her clutch. Seven perfectly formed eggs. Six are neatly tucked into the nest's central depression. One is balanced precariously on its end, pushed up against the inner wall of branches. The clutch is visible for a matter of seconds before she falls to rest once more. But where is her partner?

17 April

The air is tense. Today her movements are twitchy. She nervously scans the trees, the mud and the lake to her rear. But why? A goldfinch flits between the twigs and the pale green leaves, six feet above. A beautiful bird.

The few rays of sun which make it through the labyrinth of branches reflect off its striking red face and yellow-barred wings. An irritant perhaps, but this tiny bird and its docile nature are no threat to the pen or her clutch.

Ten feet to my left a huge family of mallard ducks skirt the lake's edge. The female lets off a loud 'quack', the male a lower, softer 'crib' as a grey heron passes over their nine tiny ducklings. A large heron could easily devour a baby duck – but the danger has passed. The swan pays no attention to the commotion behind. Her eyes are firmly fixed upon a bird in a tree to my right.

The author Samuel Orchart Beeton wrote this about the jackdaw in *Beeton's Book of Birds* (1862):

> *He is, perhaps, not quite so mischievous a bird as the magpie or the raven, but still the jackdaw must plead guilty to a large share of misdemeanours, executed with a marvellous degree of cunning.*

While tiny compared to the mute swan, the jackdaw is a real threat to her eggs. This pen has a dangerous habit of standing up, wagging her tail* and turning her back on the

---

* Ornithologists are divided as to why swans wag their tails. Some say it is solely a sign of stress. Others (myself included) have often seen swans wag their tails as they feed on bread thrown into the water, suggesting it is also a sign of excitement.

clutch. The ritual lasts only a few seconds, but that is more than enough time for this rascal to pounce.

The jackdaw is paying careful attention from his position halfway up a small willow tree. He waits for the pen to lose interest. When her head turns for just a few seconds, he hops down onto the ground, camouflaged by the tapestry of twigs, reeds, weeds and mud. He hops forward like a light-footed baby kangaroo until a metre from the nest. As the swan turns her back the jackdaw jerks forward. The swan catches a glimpse of the attack, swings her enormous neck and hisses in anger. The jackdaw, one of the world's most intelligent birds, retreats – but only by a metre. He knows the mother dare not stray too far from the nest. I stand watching for 30 minutes, the cycle repeating once, twice, three times. Each time it begins with a stare-out, the jackdaw's patience outlasting the swan's every time. While such a small bird could never flee with an egg, it could most certainly break its thin shell and devour the contents. Finally, the jackdaw gives up and disappears across the pond, empty-beaked. The cob is still nowhere to be seen.

20 April

A miserable day. Water gently rains down from the dark-grey stratus clouds, dimpling the glass-like surface of the pond. The mallards and Egyptian geese appear oblivious to the weather, rummaging through the long grass at the water's edge in search of grubs and seeds. The pen lies motionless on her nest, coiled like a sleeping snake. The canopy from the still short young trees fails to shield her from the heavy drizzle trickling onto her back from the leaves above. Every two minutes she shakes the water from her head and preens her back feathers. If she is to remain warm and transfer this heat to her treasured clutch, she must ensure that each feather is perfectly placed, each one overlapping so that the water runs off smoothly.

22 April

At last the male appears, patrolling the circular lake and dunking for weeds while keeping a vigilant lookout. Two Egyptian geese announce themselves with a loud, high-pitched 'hur-hur-hur'. The pair skim the rooftops of a nearby estate before descending onto the pond. The cob is having none of it. He curls his wings upon his back like two rip-curl waves. He dips his head, pushes down his neck towards the water and pedals furiously towards the threat. Five metres out the attack becomes more intense. He treads the water ferociously, pushes up his torso and stretches his two-metre-long wingspan, lunging at the geese, who flee to the short grass at the water's edge. He chases them across the meadow before spending the next hour guarding the two-foot-wide gap in the fence (see picture 12). At times he appears to be floating aimlessly on the sheet-flat surface. Every five minutes he lets off a soft snort to his partner hidden among the trees just five metres away. She returns the grunt.

27 April

Two weeks have passed since I began studying this nest. While wary of crows, jackdaws and magpies, the pen knows I pose no threat whatsoever. I perch nearby and watch her sleep for hours, stirring only occasionally at the squawk of a jay or the bark of a dog.

I have not seen the pen leave the nest site nor seen her eat. She looks small and weak. She works to maintain the scruffy nest, but her movements are laboured. The same cannot be said of her partner who continues patrolling the pond, hoovering up the infinite supply of bread from visiting tourists.

Today he is feeling particularly possessive, chasing away geese with increasing ferocity. I once worked out when watching a swan on a different Richmond pond that one of the best moments to photograph it is during the seconds following a successful fight. The victorious cob first lets off a gurgled snort. He then kicks his body up from the water, stretches his neck toward the sky and pounds his wings violently onto the water.

At long last, I see the pen leave the nest. But the changing of the guard is a sloppy affair. The cob is more than 20 metres (67 ft) away when he realises the nest is unoccupied. He hurries to the site, paddling through the brown water while the pen gently dunks her scruffy head down below the surface for food. When arriving he does not incubate the eggs but floats alongside, scanning the horizon like a nightclub bouncer. Thirty minutes pass before the pen returns to incubate.

8 May

The cob is in an especially aggressive mood. Usually content to chase geese from the water, today he takes more drastic action. Three greylag geese make the mistake of landing in the centre of the pond. The attack is immediate. He chases the trio from the water but one of them is too slow to escape unscathed. The straggler is pecked ferociously on the back and tail, sending feathers flying into the water. After pulling itself free, the goose reaches land but is pursued across the meadow for more than 100 metres. Only then does the swan waddle back to the water.

Whereas the cob usually reserves his aggression for geese, today nothing is safe from his wrath. He hisses and flaps at a group of small children, sending them screaming towards the safety of their parents' outstretched arms.

I make my way toward the nest, but remain a safe distance away. At first glance it seems the pen is merely restless and twitchy. She sits on the nest as usual but jerks upward every few moments as if being poked or given a small electric shock. The disturbance is coming from underneath. She leans to her left, gently lifting her right haunch to reveal a moist, gooey broken egg shell. Beside this lies a fluffy grey new-born cygnet. I can clearly make out the sticky egg substance on its back, the black pupil of its eye and the egg tooth on its bill (a tiny thorn which helps the baby pierce its way through the shell).

The mother is growing ever more restless, as if suffering from itchy underwear. She shuffles her way to her feet and forces her way through the low-lying branches towards the water's edge. The nest is exposed to reveal two more chicks, even younger than the first – wetter, slower, quieter. A fourth egg is beginning to rock from side to side, attracting the chicks' attention. I can't believe my luck. These chicks are hours, maybe minutes, old. The first is already full of boundless energy. It stumbles from one side of the nest to the other before toppling from its edge onto the muddy ground below. It then follows the mother into the brown water for its very first swim, cuddling up beside her while the remaining two chicks and four unhatched eggs are left alone and unguarded (see pictures 3–5).

The cob is busy harassing a small dog on the pond's opposite edge while the pen gently preens her brave new offspring, feeding it the tiniest pieces of weed plucked from the bed below. It's a short swim. The pen returns to the nest with chick in tow. She guides all three cygnets under her wing feathers and takes her place back upon the remaining eggs.

Surely there is nothing now that could disturb this picture of serenity?

Nurturing the young

Hatching is a quick affair lasting no more than a few hours. This is not the case for many birds, where chicks born days before their siblings have a distinct advantage. Already strong from days of feeding, these bullies prevent their smaller brothers and sisters from taking the food supplied by their parents. Somewhat callously the parents often give up on smaller chicks, investing their time and effort into offspring more likely to survive. This is rarely the case with swans. While pens may abandon eggs which have not hatched within three days of the last of the brood emerging, she will give equal attention to all of her offspring that did make it, simply because each one has the strength to demand it.

One by one the greyish-blue-tinged eggs begin gently shuddering from within. The tiny wet chicks start to tap away at the shells' membrane with their 'egg teeth'. Swan chicks are nidifugous (from the Latin meaning 'nest-fleeing') – they hatch with their eyes wide open and with fluffy waterproof white and grey down feathers. In short, they are not only adorable, but ready for action. In fact, in some cases cygnets are so eager to explore their new world, they fall from the nest just hours after hatching.

Happily, in most cases they quickly swim home or are scooped up by the pen and placed safely back inside.

This is a far cry from the plight of many other bird species, such as robins, which are altricial (meaning born undeveloped). Chicks essentially enter the world naked, without feathers and with eyes glued shut. When accidents occur – such as falling from a tree – they struggle to recover. This is not the case with lively little cygnets. Just one day after birth and a cygnet has usually discovered its oil gland towards the base of the tail. They begin the ritual of nibbling at it before spreading the greasy substance over its feathers, keeping the feathers waterproof and healthy. But exploring their own bodies does not offer as much adventure as exploring their new surroundings.

Despite the chicks' eagerness to get out and about, the pen usually waits two days before leading them to water. One big advantage to chicks fledging early is it prevents the nest from becoming infested with cygnet poo, meaning predators are less likely to track the smell.

Once safely splashed down, the next endearing chapter begins. Parent mute swans are the archetypal carers. The scene which follows is yet another visually magnificent moment revered by wildlife photographers around the globe.

The family takes to the cool water in single file, the pen leading the way while the cob guards the brood from behind. This is not just a leisurely outing, but a chance for the chicks to begin learning how to feed. At first the doting parents rip up small pieces of weed, leaving them to float on the surface towards their hungry and excitable bundles of fluff. A week later and the chicks begin dunking their heads. Three more days and they are ready to up-end, bottom in the air and head down as far as it will reach, in search of weeds.

But fending for yourself is tiring work. When exhausted, cygnets use their bills to yank themselves up onto their parents' back before settling down for a free ride in the sleepy hollows of mum and dad's feathery pillows (see picture 6).

The chicks begin communicating with their parents via a selection of 'cheeping' sounds. The more serious the situation, the louder and shriller the call. Towards the end of the first week, they even begin to practise their aggressive hisses when alarmed or threatened, and instinctively know to press themselves flat into the ground when potential threats approach. The parents respond with soft, low grunts, often loudly if the cygnets stray too far from the nest.

Such communication is of paramount importance in the weeks that follow. The chicks increasingly find and eat their own food. They grow in confidence – some might say they become cocky. They become stronger and stray farther from the nest, yet have little experience of the dangers which lie in wait from land, air and water.

The exhausted parents, who have religiously defended the nest, sometimes struggle to contain the chaos. This can be a deadly combination and means the second week of a swan's life is its most dangerous.

The following animals are all known to kill and eat cygnets: foxes, crows, magpies, jays, ravens, jackdaws, squirrels, badgers, owls, gulls, herons, snakes, mink and pike. Predators such as these help explain why the average mute swan pairing successfully raises only two chicks a year.* But if all goes well, the cygnets gradually change from soft fluffy balls of cuteness into awkward gangly adolescents over the coming months. Feathers are often uneven in length with some of them turning from a drab grey to a glistening white.

Five months pass before the young swans begin to think about their first flight. By this time they have spent many weeks flapping their increasingly strong wings while treading the water more and more aggressively. The doting parents are on hand as always, encouraging their youngsters to make dummy take-off runs, mini launches and untidy splashdowns. The many dress rehearsals eventually pay off. With the wind in their faces and the growing power generated by their increasingly strong legs and wings, the cygnets push the water away and launch themselves into the sky for the very first time. But the first

---

* Imagine if five or six survived every time. The country would be hip-deep in swans.

few flights can often be fraught with danger. I once saw a young cygnet attempt a steep turn to land in a small lake but instead become entangled in the thick branches of a nearby oak tree. Thankfully, a combination of wing flapping and branches cushioned its fall to the ground and it made a full recovery.

But practice makes perfect. As the days and weeks roll on, the cygnets become better acquainted with their new flight feathers, controlling their speed, their turns, their take-offs and their landings. It's not long before whole families are taking short flights together to visit nearby feeding grounds before returning to their territory at dusk.

But all good things must come to an end. After six months, adults expel their young (ducks do this after just one month). Sometimes this means flying back home at dusk alone, but more often it means chasing their own young away from the territory – effectively, evicting them from the family home. Parents have been known to use great violence in kicking out their own cygnets from the nesting area. It may seem cruel, but it is vital if the parents (and indeed the species) are to survive and thrive. If the cygnets remain at home, they will effectively eat the parents out of their patch. So looking ahead to next year's brood, the couple is simply doing what it must to conserve the area's food supplies. More importantly it is crucial that inbreeding does not become endemic. There is much research suggesting Canada geese have developed deformed wings because of mass inbreeding in Canada.[5]

For the offspring it must be hugely confusing. But life goes on. They spend the next 18 months moping around in familiar feeding areas, occasionally using their newfound power of flight to explore the local area. Some siblings stay together as friends – very rarely as lovers – while others disperse. Their dull, murky plumage gradually turns paler while the second year sees the bill take on a pinkish glow. It is not until the third year that most – if not all – the feathers have turned into a dazzling white. All the while, the cygnets are maturing into adults, ready to follow in their parents' footsteps. The hunt for their first partner begins.

For the parents, their work is not done. They often return to the same nesting site the following year or make it their new permanent home. If the season has been unsuccessful, they are more likely to search for a new and better location.

There is no retirement for swans – no gentle twilight years, no cruise ships and no support from their offspring. The pair is likely to stay together forever and continue breeding; learning from their successes and failures until the day one of them dies.

Perhaps it is this virtue of loyalty above all others which has drawn us towards these creatures for so many hundreds of years. History's artists, authors and poets have all been inspired by the swan's strong sense of devotion. But its romantic appeal continues to this day, and not just among birdwatchers.

When I was married, my wife could take or leave birds. As time passed we found a middle ground which accommodated my hobby without forcing us to spend too much time apart. She grew to learn I could not function without time outside, with the wind on my face and the birds in my eyes. Without birds I was simply not the person she loved.

For my part, I learned that it helped to label our birding trips as 'country strolls', to keep them short and to pepper journeys with regular tea breaks. Experience also quickly taught me it was entirely unacceptable to 'shoosh' people with an upheld hand when hearing a nuthatch singing in the distant trees.

My wife appreciated the beauty of nature but had no desire to spot a green sandpiper from a cold bird hide at Pagham Harbour or a black guillemot on the windswept shores of Portland. She grew tired when I photographed a bearded tit for hours in Croydon and a parrot crossbill in Bracknell. Yet she became obsessed with the plight of the new-born cygnets in Richmond Park. She blocked out time in her day to visit them, to feed them lettuce and take photos. She smiled at the cob's vigilance in the face of goose intruders, she giggled with joy at the plucky chicks' first clumsy steps... and then wept with sadness at their eventual demise.

———

On 9 May, the nest is empty, the cygnets gone and the eggshells crushed. That worrying habit of leaving the nest alone for short periods perhaps proved costly in the end. The squashed shells point to a fox as the most likely culprit – a reminder that nature exists not for our pleasure but because, without it, our world would not be our world.

Without baby swans we may not have foxes, and without foxes, our planet would be that little bit worse. It may appear cruel but it is not. It is just nature, the circle of life and death.

Like a child I naively returned to the scene for days in the foolish hope I was mistaken, that the fully fledged cygnets were merely hiding and would somehow emerge from the long grass into the murky shallows. I had never studied wildlife in such detail before and had never developed such a deep relationship with nature. The pair had grown to trust me at close quarters, but now I felt as though my connection to them had never existed. The aggressive and passionate energy which had radiated from this pond for so many weeks was now replaced by a palpable sense of sadness. The geese which had been so persistently hounded from the water now came and went as they pleased, no longer intimidated by the two white giants, as if smug in the knowledge that the pair had nothing left to defend. The cob and pen remained together but no longer expressed much affection, as if wallowing in their individual pain, unable to come to terms with their failure as parents and questioning the partnership itself. They continued to feed, but with a lazy demeanour, no longer ducking for weeds but inhaling the white bread tossed onto the water by tourists. Two magnificent birds, but now waning in strength, their aura dissipating further still as they left the water to scavenge a discarded sandwich – their dignity and nobility eroding before me.

I found myself not only in mourning, but in a jealous stupor at passers-by who were ignorant of the epic journey on which these swans had embarked, their struggles and their tragic end. Five days later the pen was found floating gently around the pond's edge under a pink cherry-blossom tree. Her neck was limp, her head submerged. Maybe the stress of losing her young was just too much. Her doting cob was found circling the dead body for several hours before park rangers arrived to take her away. In swans the bond is strong and the mourning long. Now that's what I call true love.

Chapter Three

THE
FIGHTER

The swan's status as a symbol of love, calm and tranquillity is beyond dispute, its standing as an icon of romance supported not only by countless stories and paintings, but by its behaviour in the wild. Time and again it has proven itself to be a standard bearer for loyalty, love and devotion.

But the swan has a darker side. It is a formidable fighter, a predator, a fiery lover, a fiercely protective parent and a violent guardian of its territory and home. Perhaps this is why the centuries have seen it used not just as an icon of love, but also as an emblem of war.

History is peppered with examples of swans being used to signify strength in battle. When the Romans, with all their naval might, began using the prows of ships as ramming weapons, the stern was nearly always decorated. Designed to curve upwards in a graceful line, it was often gilded with the head of a swan.

Then there is the medieval tale of the Knight of the Swan. This brave rescuer arrives in a boat drawn by a swan to defend a damsel. The swan towing the boat is thought to be the knight's brother, on whom his evil grandmother had cast a spell. Many suggest King Edward I founded an 'order of the swans' during his 13th-century reign. Knights were said to make their vows to the sound of trumpets in the company of two swans covered with gold bells and their necks circled with gold chains.[1]

Next there are the 11th, 16th and 28th battalions of the Australian army, which fought on the Western Front in the First World War and again in Europe and the Pacific in World War Two. When they merged to form the Royal Western Australia Regiment, the swan was chosen as its insignia under the motto 'vigilant'.

But why the swan? We have already discussed its vicious streak which, when unleashed, can be fatal. Yet the same is true of hyenas and snakes which are rarely used in coats of arms. Perhaps wily or cunning violence without quality and honour is an ugly trait unworthy of brave knights set for bloody battle in the name of crown and country. It's the *quality* which sets it apart from other violent wildlife, and the swan oozes quality.

Cruises, cosmetic brands, hotels, restaurants, football teams, insurance companies, stationery firms, vehicles and software companies have all used the noble swan's name and image to signal that their product is a cut above the rest.

It's no coincidence that the bar attached to Shakespeare's opulent Globe Theatre in London is named The Swan, nor that Disney World's most expensive hotel is crowned with two giant mute swans more than six storeys tall. As I write these words, my mum is shouting out 'Swarovski'. She's right of course. The glamorous jewellery company features a swan as its logo. An hour later a Sipsmith gin advert appears on TV featuring an animated swan. The commercial again points to the product's superior quality and ends with the tagline: 'We make gin, not compromises'.

Then there are Swan Vestas matches which British smokers have used to light their puffers for more than 130 years. The product tagline now reads: 'Made to the highest quality since 1883.' As the author Peter Young quite rightly points out, 'a strong bird, it builds strong brands'.

Once again, we find ourselves discussing the contradictions of the swan. Adorning Valentine's cards and expensive jewellery but also inspiring bravery and strength in bloody battle. This dual personality has been portrayed in ancient myths and folklore for many hundreds of years.

Stories outlining these contradictions have been found in Greek, Roman, Celtic, Scandinavian and Native American cultures, among others. Many tales feature humans switching between the beautiful and the destructive using feathered cloaks with magical powers. But in the everyday world it is the breeding season which sees the swan don the cloak of aggression. It can be savagely violent when its mate or offspring is under threat. Sometimes this fury is directed toward other swans, but often its target is other birds, animals and, on occasion, humans.

Swans vs nature

Is the swan a predator? The word 'predator' is surely one of the most misunderstood terms in nature. Predators are often assumed to be large mammals such as tigers and lions or smaller but aggressive life forms such as spiders and snakes. You rarely hear a dolphin described as a predator, nor a penguin, but they all behave in the same way: hunting down their terrified prey before killing and devouring it without mercy.

The term 'bird of prey' is misleading, implying that birds outside families such as hawks, eagles, falcons and harriers have no interest in capturing, killing and eating prey. This of course could not be further from the truth. As I write these words, I am watching a male blackbird mutilating and devouring an earthworm on a chilly, damp spring morning. We rightly sentimentalise its song but forget the killing that sustains it. A pair of blue tits is also busy murdering a row of ants creeping among the small branches of the garden's birch tree.

I much prefer the word 'raptor' when referring to our more glamourous bird hunters, such as sparrowhawks, kestrels and golden eagles. Derived from the Latin word *rapio* – meaning 'to seize by force' – it explains that 'force' is required to catch its prey – something the ant-picking blue tit can survive without. The British Trust for Ornithology clears things up nicely by stressing that raptors are distinguished from other winged hunters by their propensity for hunting vertebrates which are 'large relative to the hunter'. In other words, a huge amount of relative force is required to take down the prey.

We can therefore label the swan a predator but not a raptor. Although it is more than happy to spend its day munching on a variety of weeds and grasses, it is also partial to the occasional insect, snail or fish egg. Swans have even been known to target small fish or tadpoles. But this is not where the swan earns its reputation as a formidable fighter. People who have spent any time near Britain's waterways will have witnessed an angry swan in action. They usually attack for one of three reasons: to fend off a love rival, to defend territory or to defend offspring. Some of the world's most spectacular bird fights are contested by male mute swans. Once a male has found a mate, he will defend her jealously. Once a father, he will violently attack anything which threatens his cygnets. And once he has secured a territory he will fight to the death to protect it.

A battle over territory with an intruding swan usually begins with an intimidating head-on approach. The male swims faster than usual toward the intruder, punching through the water with fast and powerful foot strokes beneath the surface. Above board he raises the elbows, forming a graceful arch over the back. He throws back his head but pushes his neck down toward the water to form the famous 'busking posture', similar to a coiled cobra ready to pounce.

Once the gladiators meet, the defender turns side-on to the intruder, lowers his head, hisses, and begins swinging the head from side to side. The two swans then begin fighting head-on, attacking one another with powerful wings and bills. In keeping with many forms of combat, both struggle to gain the higher ground by towering above the other. The pair's necks become entangled as they rain down fearsome blows with their huge arms.

The goal here is simple – to injure the combatant or push its head underwater until they drown, which they often do. Around four per cent of cobs are thought to die from battles over territory.

One example leaps out more than most. A killer swan, affectionately named Hannibal, was relocated after killing 15 other birds. Hannibal, who laid claim to the grounds of Wales's Pembroke Castle, attacked anything which strayed into his territory. Wildlife worker Maria Evans, who worked at the castle's pond, told the *Daily Telegraph* in September 2010: 'I have never come across such an aggressive bird. He is an absolutely horrible swan and people really don't like him. I've lost count of the times I've been to pick up dead and injured swans.'

Her colleague Ruth Harrison told the newspaper: 'Afterwards he swims around the pond with his wings up looking so proud of what he has done. If his victims are injured on the bank, he just won't let them back in the water.' In the end, conservationists removed Hannibal and his family from the pond to be settled elsewhere, where he's no doubt terrorising any swan that dares come his way.[2]

Defeated intruders who *are* lucky enough to escape with their lives usually withdraw their wings in a submissive pose and flee. The victor returns to his mate where the pair often celebrate with a series of loud, triumphant snorts while gently rubbing breasts and necks. They then rise up from the water and flap their wings in a display of power.

Battles for territory with non-breeding swans, or youngsters, are far less brutal. These contests can be easily mistaken for a dance, with the two half-hearted warriors rising up and flapping their wings in each other's general direction. In some cases the female joins in before the brief encounter usually fizzles out into nothing. But attacks on a swan's cygnets are a much more serious affair.

Swans will do almost anything to protect their young and have been known to trample the eggs of other water birds who nest too close. In most cases, however, it is the bird's wing which causes the damage. Similar to humans, swans have an upper arm, a lower arm, an elbow and a wrist. A bony knuckle forms the bend of the wing. This joint helps form a defensive shield but also acts as a bludgeon in combat.

Even humans are vulnerable to the aggression of swans during the breeding season. In June 2019, the *Guardian* newspaper reported how students and tourists were being constantly attacked by a swan on Cambridge's River Cam. This particular swan, mischievously named Asbaby (after ASBO – Anti Social Behaviour Order), took a particular dislike to drunken students celebrating exam success by jumping into the water.

But while comical tales such as this are commonplace in the spring and summer months, there has been at least once incident which ended in genuine tragedy. Probably the most famous case of swan aggression towards perceived intruders occurred in the United States. According to ABCNews.com, one morning in April 2012 Anthony Hensley was kayaking on a pond in Chicago when he was attacked by a swan which pushed him into the water. The 37-year-old fought to resurface, but the swan continued to push his head down until he drowned. Mr Hensley worked on the property and was checking in on the birds. It is thought he paddled too close to the nest.

Swans vs dogs

Swans become massively agitated around cats and dogs – particularly during the breeding season. Countless examples exist of playful dogs jumping into the water, excited by the misguided expectation of frolicking and splashing around with a big white bird. However, the scene can easily take a sour turn. Desperate to protect their offspring, the parent (usually the cob) will often attack the dog, holding it underwater with powerful wings – sometimes until it drowns.

In May 2004, upon seeing a Springer Spaniel swimming and chasing its cygnets, a cob lunged forward, battering the dog with its wings and pecking aggressively. The dazed mutt was pinned underwater. Two minutes later the dog's lifeless body floated to the surface before the eyes of his distraught owner, who had been screaming from the water's edge.[3]

More recently, in July 2019 a Cocker Spaniel suffered a similar fate. After jumping into a pond in Dublin's Bushy Park, it swam towards a group of cygnets. The cob attacked, once again pinning the pooch underwater with its powerful wings until it stopped struggling – and breathing.[4]

The truth remains that dogs and cats do a lot more damage to swans than the other way around. Dogs commonly trample over eggs or kill cygnets. They occasionally attack and kill adult birds. Making sure that dogs are kept on a lead and that cats wear bell collars is the easiest way to protect both pet and swan.

Swans vs hunters

Swans are intelligent birds. When treated with respect, they have the capacity to learn and to trust. In the absence of a mother or father, a cygnet will accept the first large moving object it sees as its parent – a cat, a dog, a farmyard hen, or indeed a human being. In the numerous cases where people have rescued swan chicks left orphaned or rejected, the babies have usually accepted human fostering and become entirely devoted. It is perhaps for this reason that man and swan have been able to live happily together since the days of ancient Greece.

Mute swans have been domesticated for thousands of years. Their trust in humans over so many centuries may help explain why they have developed semi-domesticated personality traits, seeking bread from people, staying close to built-up areas and sharing waterways with our boats. Sadly, humans have also been responsible for betraying this trust with unforgivable crimes. We have destroyed their habitat, poisoned their waters and in some cases committed acts of sick and twisted vandalism.

———

It is likely that men in Britain first hunted swans soon after arriving on these islands around 900,000 years ago. Swans were easy targets. They were big, slow and particularly vulnerable when moulting and unable to fly.

During the period from 8,000 to 3,000 BCE, when hunting weapons became more sophisticated (bows and arrows, latterly with copper tips), swans, ducks, cormorants, goldeneyes and jays were hunted en masse.[5] By around 500 BCE, during the Iron Age, swans were starting to be revered. Myths and legends were passed down about the bird's supernatural powers (more on that in the next chapter). This did not stop people eating them.

When the Romans arrived in 55 BCE with their swords, spears and catapults, the slaughter escalated still further. These latest invaders were most likely the first to begin domesticating swans, farming them for meat along with greylag geese and ducks. Fossils of all three of Britain's native swan species have been found in Colchester dating back to between 43 CE and 400 CE. The Normans are thought to have used similar domesticating methods, as did the Vikings before them.

Meanwhile, swan farming methods developed in the Middle Ages and hunting also increased in technical knowhow. Humans used boats, horses, dogs and a variety of weapons as well as nets and traps to hunt them. It really was a grim time for swans. But in 1191, when Richard I returned triumphant from his conquest of Cyprus, there was at least some good news for London's swan population. He arrived home with hundreds of mute swans he had taken from the Mediterranean island specifically to adorn the Thames, declaring them protected. Many people to this day mistakenly believe it was Richard who introduced swans to our shores.

But probably the biggest triumph for swans came nearly 300 years later with Edward IV's 1482 Act for Swans. With the stroke of a pen, all mute swans were made the property of either the king or wealthy landowners.

Hunting had effectively become the preserve of the rich and the crown, increasing the odds of survival for swans who could stay clear of both.

Those who couldn't continued to be exploited by their wealthy owners, as swans had uses for humans beyond a mere source of food. Flight feathers were used with hats and fans, while swan quills were thought to make better-quality, and longer-lasting, pens than the quills of goose feathers. Queen Elizabeth I found another use for swans when touring the country during her reign. Hosts of the monarch were instructed to provide bedding and upholstery made from feathers plucked from swans in the Thames.[6] But one of the most novel uses for the feathers was in removing bees from a honeycomb. This delicate procedure required a tool softer than a paint brush that caused no harm to the bees and did not allow them to crawl between the bristles. The flight feathers were also used in 'marbling', where objects were coloured with flowing patterns to give a marbled, vein-like effect.[7]

It would seem that almost no part of the swan went to waste. Bones were used for tools, beads, whistles, drinking tubes and pipes.[8] Skins were combined with feathers to make feather boas and ladies' powder puffs, while the feet were rubbed with grease and converted into tobacco pouches and purses.

Strangely, it was the Second World War which put an end to swan farming by wealthy landowners in Britain.

A shortage of the swan's main food (grain) meant that it was no longer a viable business model. The practice had already long been in decline, with tastier birds, such as turkeys, readily available since the sixteenth century and requiring less effort to rear, prepare and cook.

In modern times, swans have come up against an equally formidable foe in the form of fishermen. In 1961 the Home Office was lobbied by anglers and farmers to act on what was an increasing number of wild swans. Fishermen argued that swans were destroying the weeds needed to provide cover for fish (and their bait). Farmers meanwhile complained that swans were munching away huge swathes of oilseed rape, spring grazing grass and cereals.

The Wildfowl Trust and the British Trust for Ornithology were asked to estimate swan numbers in Britain and landed on the somewhat bizarre figure of 'between 17,850 and 19,250'.[9] The government concluded that swans were causing negligible damage to livelihoods. There was plenty of weed to meet the needs of both swans and fishermen. And farmers? Well, they were welcome to use small explosive bangers or electric fences to protect their land. No action was to be taken to reduce swan numbers, unless populations jumped considerably.

But no sooner had the government acted to defend the swan than nature struck a deadly blow on the fishermen's behalf. The winter of 1962/63 was cruel and hard. Temperatures rarely rose above –2 °C (28.4 °F), and blizzards caused havoc. Waterways and lakes were frozen solid. Thousands of swans were left unable to duck and dive for their treasured weed. They simply starved to death.

It was shortly after the big freeze that the Wildfowl Trust began investing heavily in 'bird ringing': the act of catching birds and placing an identifying ring around a leg to enable the rangers to monitor their progress. One consequence of more data was a new awareness of previously unsuspected problems. Of the 2,156 dead, ringed swans recovered between 1960 and 1965, conservationists could only ascertain the cause of death in the cases of 1,051 birds. The rest were a mystery. They noted that an abnormally high proportion of the unexplained deaths belonged to young swans, but needed to get a clearer picture of what was happening. Could the young deaths be explained by the perils of youth – vulnerability to predators and naivety when searching for food? No. A short investigation found the largest cause of death was not starvation, not entanglement from fishing wires, not predation, but collisions with overhead cables.

Swans vs pylons

April 1996
I am birdwatching with a friend near Newbury Racecourse in Berkshire. It is a crisp, chilly spring morning with the

sun reflecting off the dewy grass. We make our way up a shallow hill on a wide tractor track bordered by dense hedges – a mixture of bramble, nettles and baby birches. The meadow to our left is scruffy and uneven, a mix of lush field grass and tougher, longer ryegrass. These larger tufts are a foot in height, scattered between scores of molehills, a magnet for myriad flies searching for a sip of dewy water. For the swallows and house martins, recently arrived from Africa, it is like shooting fish in a barrel. They dance and dive at these larger, muddier tufts – gobbling up the bluebottles and house flies before blasting back up into the sky and swooping downwards to complete circuit after circuit.

Up above, a skylark is singing its sublime tune – the song of springtime – an endless outpouring of high rolling notes, quiet at first, but louder as it floats back down towards Earth. One of my late grandad's favourites, this small unspectacular-looking bird will always have a special place in my heart. When tidying his bedroom shortly after his death, I found a small metal box from his time in the army during the Second World War. It was packed full of clippings from magazines and books. One ripped page featured a poem by John Clare describing the challenge of spotting a skylark in the sunny open skies:

And o'er her half-formed nest, with happy wings
Winnows the air, till in the cloud she sings,

Then hangs a dust-spot in the sunny skies,
And drops, and drops, till in her nest she lies,
Which they unheeded passed—not dreaming then
That birds which flew so high would drop agen
To nests upon the ground, which anything
May come at to destroy. Had they the wing.

The skylark is the king of the songbirds. In this view, I am not alone. Samuel Orchart Beeton wrote in 1862:

> *As the lion is the king of the beasts, so*
> *may the skylark claim the monarchy of*
> *the musical feather tribes......*
> *Higher and higher he mounts till he*
> *seems no bigger than a bee, still the music*
> *of his tiny throat, no more capacious*
> *than a little reed, fills the broad expanse,*
> *and is sweetly audible to us as we stand*
> *in the cornfield, with our head thrown*
> *back, and our eyes shaded by our hands,*
> *lest we altogether lose sight of the*
> *quivering speck among the motes that*
> *float in the sunbeams.*

As I watch the skylark down below, another songbird takes centre stage. Seemingly oblivious to the opera in the skies, a male blackbird perches on an abandoned plough.

With its dark corners, nooks and crannies, this rusting wreck is the perfect nesting home for Britain's third-favourite bird.

Just 30 feet above, a kestrel sits atop an electricity pylon. Clearly not in hunting mode, he soaks up the morning sun. Its small grey head leans to the right – giving the occasional glance downwards at the stubble and activity below. After two minutes the bird drifts down but then uses the wind to glide back up toward the woods. It follows the same arc, its wings kinking and straightening in steady beats, before dropping back to the pole on which until a minute earlier it had perched. Irate jackdaws are worried by the presence of the kestrel, circling the pole like flies bothering a cow.

To our right, a narrow footpath diverges from the track in the direction of a bird hide. The path is framed by hawthorn bushes and budding birch and cherry blossom trees – home to chaffinches, goldcrests, greenfinches and, best of all, bullfinches. The hide is a Berkshire ornithological hotspot, looking down upon a gravel pit which a wide array of waders, gulls, ducks and pipits call home. But now is not the time for sitting in a hide. The weather outside is too crisp and fresh. We are busy skulking our way up the track in search of two yellow wagtails. At first, they flew overhead, calling with their shrill 'pseet' before disappearing toward the foot of a bramble hedge. As we turn in a gentle bend to the right, we spot the pair pecking at insects on the edge of the track. A horse has clearly been up here in the last few hours, leaving a tasty treat for a swarm of flies.

We stalk the wagtails, desperate to approach them undetected. The author J. A. Baker's words are once again ringing in my ears, tales of his quiet search for peregrine falcons fresh in the mind. 'Hide the white tremor of the hands' – my gloves are neatly worn. 'Shade the stark reflecting face' – my scarf and hat are pulled up and down. 'Let your shape grow, but do not alter its outline' – we could not be approaching any slower. 'To share fear is the greatest bond of all' – we try to put ourselves in the skin of the wagtails.

As I bring my binoculars up to my face, the wagtails flee skyward and out of sight. A second later, from behind us we hear a sickening blow. A simultaneous thump, a hiss and a twang – the frightful noise of a visibly vibrating pylon cable which turns my stomach and jars my neck in fright.

As we stare to our left, the scene is now bereft of birdlife. No kestrel, no blackbird, no swallows – all spooked by the horrible noise. Only the flies remain – now uninterested in the moist blades of grass, their attention turned towards a far greater prize.

—

Swans are ill equipped to deal with overhead cables. Eyes placed on the side of the head give them a wide field of vision, a bit like a radar, helping to spot predators attacking from almost any direction (nearly 360 degrees). The sacrifice is a limited frontal vision. The two monocular fields of sight in either eye combine at the front to produce a single narrow image, leaving them not just vulnerable to thin wires but to camouflaged buildings, bridges and cliff faces too (see picture 15).

Their frame and wings are also poorly suited to last-second changes of direction. A swan's wingspan is enormous, sometimes greater than the length of the bird. They have been known to simultaneously touch two live cables, blacking out entire villages before dropping dead from electrocution. More commonly, the impact with even a single wire brings death or horrendous injury.

The structure of the wings – long, wide and slow-beating – has evolved for long migrations but is poor in terms of manoeuvrability. Even if a swan were to spot the wire, there is no guarantee it would be able to swerve or dip in time.

I will never know whether this elegant animal saw the wire before colliding with it on this fresh spring morning in Newbury. It wasn't ringed, and without a ring we can't even speculate about its origin or likely destination. But we can appraise how long it had lived before being felled by one of the many deadly human obstacles that modern swans have to negotiate.

This was a large bird – a thick neck but not yet the pure white colour that would mark it as fully mature. Perhaps a nomadic male, looking for a mate or maybe an adolescent scouring the area for new feeding grounds? We know that two-year-old male swans tend to move around a lot, seeking out food and mates. How sad that it was only months, maybe even weeks, from breeding.

The Wildfowl Trust's study after the big freeze of 1962/63 proved that swans around this age are more susceptible to pylon deaths. Migrating in search of their first breeding grounds, two-year-old swans are more mobile than most. Very few ever survive such a collision and never get the chance to learn from past mistakes. This swan had a quick death – its head was pointing at a grotesque angle, a grisly sight, but at least a broken neck brings a speedy end.

As we watch the twitching body quickly come to rest, we vow to join the RSPB. Nothing will bring this young swan back to our skies and waterways, but maybe we can contribute towards protecting its habitat. With more suitable unspoiled terrain nearby, perhaps it would never have felt the need to take off. Over the coming days we return to the scene, stumbling in the field's sticky mud.

Next morning: The eyes have been removed, probably by a crow or magpie. Flies (mostly bluebottles) are focussing on the extremities – tail, eyeholes, feet and inner bill.

Day 2: The head is missing. Likely a fox. Outer feathers are intact and clean.

Day 3: Neck clearly decomposing from the top down, the body being eaten from the inside out. Feathers slightly dishevelled.

Day 4: The neck looks like it has been pressed into the ground with a hot iron. Maggots visible. Some organs exposed. Feet missing. Rancid smell – like rotten eggs with garlic.

Day 5: Carcass has moved six feet. Neck remains 'pressed' to the ground in the original location. A mammal of some kind, probably a fox, has tried and failed to take the body. Some feathers removed, exposing the rotting skin.

Day 6: Carcass has moved a further ten feet. More feathers removed. Body significantly smaller.

Day 7: Carcass has disappeared. Trail of feathers leading into nearby woodland.

Days 8–10: Swan feathers (large and small) being collected by blackbirds and wood pigeons for nesting material.

Day 12: All feathers have disappeared.

If there is one shred of comfort it is that the swan's death was not in vain. A full spectrum of wildlife has benefited from its demise. The flies and maggots are prey for smaller birds, the smaller birds are prey for sparrowhawks.

The body itself is food for a troop of foxes, while its feathers will furnish the homes of an array of new-born birdlife in the coming weeks.

Thankfully, telecommunication and electricity companies now make good efforts to limit the danger. Diverters (brightly coloured plastic discs) now adorn most cables in high-risk areas.* Attempts are also being made to avoid erecting cables along known migration routes.[10]

In recent times it is the growing use of windfarms causing problems. Swans can collide with the turbines' arms or become entangled in the farms' supporting cables in mist or fog. The most high-profile bird death of this nature occurred in 2013 on Scotland's Isle of Harris. White-throated needletails look like a cross between a swift, a swallow and a house martin. They are usually found in Asia or Australasia, particularly in places like Japan, Siberia or Australia. Commonly seen in large numbers during the hours before a thunderstorm, locals call them 'storm birds'. Needletails feed on a range of insects from beetles and flies to bees and moths. Hot air rises during warm, dry weather, sometimes taking these critters hundreds of feet into the sky. But during cold or humid weather the same insects stick closer to the ground in search of shelter. During those moist, muggy moments

* The cables on this particular day *were* marked with orange discs. On this occasion, they did not have the desired effect but may have prevented other accidents.

before a thunderstorm, the needletail skims the surface, hastily gobbling insects before the rain begins to fall. Storm birds.

Why this particular needletail was flying alone in the Outer Hebrides in mid-June remains a mystery. These birds migrate from the Indian subcontinent to nest in Siberia and central Asia. Scotland's RSPB could only assume it overshot its migratory course and found itself flying above the Norwegian Sea. Perhaps the Isle of Harris was the first dry land it found.

Around 40 birdwatchers, some from as far away as Surrey in southeast England, made the journey to see a species recorded only five times in the UK since 1955. But as the twitchers huddled together in the cold to watch this incredible bird duck and dive at speeds of 105mph, their pilgrimage ended in a terrible spectacle.

The town of Drinishader features a single wind turbine atop a rocky knoll. As the needletail swooped round on a feeding run, one of the turbine's three mighty arms came spinning around, striking a deadly blow. The Rare Bird Alert, an online service notifying users of rare birds, had passed on reports to birdwatchers and twitchers across the UK. In a tweet, the service now announced: 'The white-throated needletail on Harris flew into a wind turbine and has died, pathetic way for such an amazing bird to die.'

A spokeswoman for RSPB Scotland told BBC News: 'Whilst the collision is very unfortunate, incidents of this sort are really very rare. Careful choice of location and design of windfarms and turbines prevents, as much as possible, such occurrences happening on a large scale.' She also rightly pointed out that 'Wind energy makes a vital contribution towards mitigating the impacts of climate change, which is the biggest threat to our native birds and wildlife.'

The bird's body was later sent to a museum. While few nature enthusiasts would decry the expansion of cleaner energy sources, it is vital that action is taken to mitigate the risk that individual units pose to birds in particular. Illuminating turbines with flashing lights is not the answer. Experts suggest this would attract rather than deter the birds, increasing the risk of collision. Efforts can be made to ensure enormous farms are not placed along migration routes – especially as swans and other birds fly low when making short journeys or beginning or ending long ones – particularly in mist and fog. But while our birds face many dangers in the sky, a vast array of perils exist on the ground too.

One of the more bizarre threats to swans is roads, though not in the way you might assume. Swans in the UK have been known to land on wet shiny roads, mistakenly thinking the tarmac strip is a river. If they are lucky enough to avoid oncoming traffic, they are often left with nasty grazes on their feet. Highways staff are trained to capture them safely.[11]

Swans vs fishermen

The big freeze of 1962/63 was not the only crisis faced by swans during the swinging 60s. No sooner had the battle with the cold ended than the battle with the fishermen resumed. It continues to this day.

Birds too often become entangled in abandoned fishing lines causing awful injuries to their legs and wings. Many are left as flightless 'one wingers'. In some cases, the nylon lines become so tightly wrapped around the bill that the swan is prevented from eating. When abandoned hooks or fishing tackle are swallowed, the inner throat is sliced and the bill cut, once again leaving the bird at risk of starvation unless rescued. Thankfully deaths from fishing tackle decreased considerably in the 1990s and 2000s – not because of fewer hooks or lines, but due to a very subtle rule change.

Lead is both heavy and soft. It can be easily ground down by a swan's bill and swallowed, entering the bloodstream. Eating as few as three pellets is enough to paralyse a swan's oesophageal muscles, preventing food from reaching the stomach and leading to starvation. Worse still, the problem can be passed on to offspring. Cygnets born with high levels of lead in their blood are less likely to mature.

In 1979 the Labour Minister of State for the Environment, Denis Howell, asked the Nature Conservancy Council to investigate the deaths of mute swans on Stratford's River Avon. The group discovered that lead used in the anglers' weights was poisoning the water. The government ruled these weights should be withdrawn in five years. Independent research undertaken around this time suggested around 3,400–4,200 swans were dying each year from lead poisoning – mostly caused by fishermen.[12]

Non-toxic weights were developed during the following five years, giving fishermen the chance to phase out their soon-to-be-illegal tools. Thankfully, while not completely eradicated, rescue centres now see far fewer deaths from lead poisoning.

Swans vs oil

Oil spills seemed to be an almost annual event during my childhood. I remember, aged seven, hearing of an explosion on the oil tanker *Odyssey* which spilled 132,000 tonnes of oil into the ocean near Nova Scotia, Canada in 1988. Because of the distance from land, thankfully very little ecological damage was reported. But just months later the *Exxon Valdez* struck a reef in Alaska's Prince William Sound, spilling more than 100,000 tonnes of its oily cargo into the Gulf of Alaska. Immediate deaths included 100,000 to 250,000 seabirds – guillemots, auks and ducks. At least 2,800 sea otters perished as well as 12 river otters, 300 harbour seals,

247 bald eagles and 22 orcas. That's before we even begin to count the fish.

Next came distressing images of helpless pelicans and lapwings suffering at the hands of Iraqi dictator Saddam Hussein. In January 1991, with his back to the wall from Allied advances, the Iraqi president used pollution as a tactic of war for the first time in history. Early reports pointed the finger at US bombing raids on two oil tankers, but it soon became clear Hussein had ordered the oil valves of a sea island pipeline to be opened. The result was 240 million gallons of crude oil flowing into the Persian Gulf. The apparent aim was to hinder or prevent US Marines from launching an invasion from the sea. It is impossible to know the scale of the devastation on surrounding eco-systems; it's not as if a team of conservationists could fly to the scene. But we do know the impact on marine life was truly awful and that huge swathes of the coastline are still uninhabitable.

But the oil disaster which had the biggest impact on my view of the world was the *Braer* oil spill in the Shetland Islands, which happened in January 1993, when I was 11 years old. I remember my school class was asked to sit down in front of a TV. Mrs Roberts told us the images we were about to see were very sad. We could leave the room if we wanted – it was our choice. I recall two distinct emotions. Firstly, pride. I was being trusted to decide for myself whether I could watch. It reminded me of a time I was offered veal at a buffet dinner in Majorca. My dad explained to me the farming methods surrounding calves in Spain and left me with the choice.*

But as footage of rows of black, limp, glossy carcasses were laid out on the beach, I felt a deep sense of sadness and a pang of shame. Many of the dead, greasy birds washed up on the shores of this northernmost part of my own country were species I had never seen. They were 'unticked' in my children's *Spotter's Guide*. The thick black bodies piling up in front of the TV cameras were unrecognisable from the illustrations I had studied as a kid.

We had an excellent primary-school teacher. She asked what we knew about oil. Our experiences were chiefly cans of oil in our dads' garages – used to grease up our BMXs. A couple of the kids mentioned car mechanics.

As Mrs Roberts gently, and without judgement, explained our role in the demand for oil via cars, electricity and more, I began to realise my birdwatching could come to mean more than just ticking birds off a list. In this instance, the Shetland oil disaster, a crude-oil tanker, the *Braer*, had run aground off the Shetland Islands in hurricane-force winds, spilling almost 85,000 tonnes of oil into the North Sea and Atlantic Ocean. Coastguards were first alerted to a problem at around 5 a.m. on 3 January when the 240-metre-long

---

* I ate it – and regret it to this day. (More on meat-eating hypocrisy in Chapter Four – The Myth)

tanker lost power in high winds en route from Norway to Canada. At this stage it was still ten miles from the southern tip of the Shetland Islands but slowly the enormous vessel drifted northwards until it crashed into the rocks.

Fortunately, the impact on wildlife was not as devastating as the *Exxon Valdez* disaster just four years earlier. Firstly, winds blew much of the oil out to sea rather than towards a coastline saturated with sea birds and mammals. Secondly, the *Braer* was carrying Gulfaks crude oil, thought to be significantly lighter and more biodegradable than that which flowed from the stricken Exxon ship. Still, according to the World Wide Fund for Nature (WWF), up to 32,000 birds are estimated to have died in the Braer disaster, with nearly a quarter of the local grey seal population either contaminated or killed. The vast majority of bird victims were cormorants, guillemots, shags and puffins. Only a few coastal mute swans are thought to have been affected.

The same could not be said in 1956 when an oil barge sank in the River Thames at Battersea. This saw 243 mute swans perish, decimating the local population, which took years to recover. At Burton-on-Trent a flock of 90 moulting swans was cut to just 15 following another major spill on the River Trent in the same year.[13]

But why is oil so damaging? The charity International Bird Rescue explains that spills can lead to three different types of death.

The first relates to feathers. Crude oil essentially causes feathers to mat and to separate, exposing the skin and the body to the cold. For seabirds, who are more commonly the victims of oil spills, this is devastating. The body is no longer protected from the icy water. Hypothermia quickly ensues, followed by death.

But even less saturated birds will begin obsessively preening to rid themselves of this nasty substance. Some ingest too much, causing their internal organs to shut down. Others spend so much time preening that they forget to eat, they grow weaker and become more susceptible to predators.

Finally, for the birds most badly affected, the sticky oil renders their feathers unresistant to water and they simply sink and drown. Some more fortunate birds are washed up on shore and rescued by concerned citizens or capture crews from rescue charities. The rescuers clean off the oil in a long and intricate process divided into five stages – washing, rinsing, drying, waterproofing and releasing. It's a process often used on swans which stray into oil slicks.

The damaged bird goes through a series of 'tub washes' with a low concentration of a substance similar to washing-up liquid. Tiny brushes are used to dislodge the oil. Next, rinsing is of vital importance because, without this, the washing-up liquid is just as damaging as the oil. Special spa nozzles are used to propel the water at sufficient pressure to remove all traces of detergent. The clean bird is then placed in a padded area with gentle pet-grooming dryers. Hopefully by this stage it will have started safely preening its feathers back into place. It is also tube-fed a nutritious food mixture to help build up strength. When completely dry, the bird is placed in a warm-water therapy pool. Rescuers closely monitor its progress, checking its ability to float and to swim. The water therapy and drying process is then repeated until the bird is healthy, waterproof and ready for release back into the wild.

Swans vs vandals

The struggles and threats faced by swans are wide and varied. Those we have discussed so far have involved swans being the innocent victims of humankind's clumsiness, irresponsibility or recklessness. Humans can be selfish, ignorant and show disregard for other creatures in the pursuit of better food, homes or lifestyle, but these cases do not include acts of wanton violence or sadism. Sadly, on top of discarded lead weights, pieces of fishing line, power cables and oil spills, there is a more deliberate hazard in the form of people willing to do harm for the sake of it.

In modern-day Britain, hunting is largely a thing of the past. But swans continue to suffer at the hands of mindless vandals. Springtime often brings horror stories of nests being ravaged by thugs throwing stones and bottles, often killing the young or breaking the eggs. In April 2019, the *Shropshire Star* reported how vandals had smashed six swan eggs with bricks on the moat of Whittington Castle. When police removed the bricks, the pen returned to gently remove the shells from the nest.

In 2011, the *Bucks Free Press* revealed how mute swans in Reading, Windsor and Marlow were being subjected to regular attacks from vandals using air rifles and catapults. Many of the swans were left with devastating injuries to the eyes and jaw. Others swam away wounded before eventually drowning.

In the summer of 2020, news broke of a spate of swan attacks in my Berkshire hometown of Thatcham. Thugs with air rifles had targeted nesting swans. Five had been shot in the area in the space of ten days. One died. Local attention, however, focused on the plight of a female who had been shot while incubating four eggs on a nest beside a lake across the road from my childhood home. The 8 mm (0.3 in.) ball-shaped pellet struck the helpless pen an inch behind the eye and lodged in her skull.

Rescuers from the rehabilitation centre, Swan Support, hurried to the scene and took her to their headquarters in Datchet. The following day she was moved to a nearby vet for emergency surgery to remove the pellet. Ten days later, the pen was ready to be returned to the lake in which she was shot. Rescuers filmed the moment she was welcomed back by her loving partner. After gingerly waddling into the shallow water, she brushes past the long green grass and gently paddles towards the cob. A willow warbler and chiffchaff can be heard singing in the background. The male lets off a loud snort before the pair begin a dance of love, gently turning their heads from side to side in unison. The ritual lasts about ten seconds before they return to the crucial job of foraging for weeds. (You can watch the video on my website, at www.ilikebird.uk/shot-swan).

Swan Support operations director Wendy Hermon told me the moment was 'a beautiful thing to see – the best part of the job', but that she was disgusted that some people get joy from using swans as target practice. It seems that school holidays often see an upsurge in these types of attacks. Wendy explained: 'Summer and, obviously, the coronavirus lockdown were really bad. I guess kids get bored. Christmas is bad as well, maybe kids have new air rifles or catapults as presents.' Unsurprisingly, while the pen made a full recovery, her clutch of eggs died during the time she was away.

More tragedy unfolded just weeks later – this time in west London's usually peaceful Richmond Park. Royal Parks Police – a division of the Metropolitan Police – issued an appeal for information to catch a male jogger seen kicking a cygnet on a footpath on 8 June at 5.30 p.m, rather than change his course. The Swan Sanctuary in Shepperton, Surrey, swooped in to treat the bird at its medical centre but were unable to save it from fatal internal injuries.

Other vandals are happy to attack our wildfowl with paint, affecting their ability to fly and swim. The RSPCA has even been called out to rescue a swan suffering from burns after a fisherman poured a flask of hot coffee over its head.

Quite what goes through people's minds when they commit such acts of savagery will remain a mystery to most of us. Thankfully the vast majority of people are kind, caring and protective of our swans, our birds and our natural world.

A licence to kill

Bizarrely, recent years have seen wildlife campaigners locking horns with a public body who are ostensibly tasked with 'promoting nature conservation'. In 2019 it was reported that Natural England, funded by the Department for Environment, Food and Rural Affairs, had issued licences to destroy 170,000 wild birds, eggs and nests over five years. While wild birds and their nests are protected under the Wildlife and Countryside Act 1981, licences can be sought to kill birds and destroy nests if they are found to be seriously damaging farming, fishing and forestry interests or endangering people's health and safety.

Many of these 'licences to kill' included rare and declining species such as curlews and swifts. Peregrine falcons, barn owls, buzzards and red kites were on the list, as well as garden favourites such as robins, blackbirds and blue tits. The *Guardian* newspaper homed in on the case of a licence even being issued to destroy a wren's nest to 'preserve public safety' in South Yorkshire. Greylag geese (67,586 licences), mallard ducks (21,939), herring gulls (16,052) and cormorants (12,033) attracted the most licences, but swans were not immune.

In Wiltshire, a licence was issued to destroy 300 mute swans' eggs to prevent 'serious damage to growing timber'. Licensed methods for killing swans include shooting and trapping and destroying nests by hand. Pricking eggs or dousing them in liquid paraffin to prevent hatching are also approved methods.

Despite protests from the likes of TV presenter Chris Packham and wildlife campaigner Mark Avery, Natural England does not publish details for each and every licence. A Natural England spokesperson told the *Guardian* that although all wild birds are protected by law, there are certain circumstances, such as to protect the public from harm, where licences can be issued for bird control under the Wildlife and Countryside Act 1981. He added that the 'number of birds that may be killed is strictly limited and won't harm the conservation status of any species'.

Hope

Despite all of this, it is crucial to remember that people have fought to protect these glorious birds and will continue to do so. The big freeze of 1962/63 may well have decimated huge swathes of birds, but hundreds of swans were saved by the kindness of strangers who braved the ice and snow to deliver them food.

Probably the most emotive example I have witnessed of the potential of humans and swans to live in peace and friendship involves the bell-ringing swans of the Bishop's Palace in Wells. Swans have lived on the palace's moats since the 1850s and are famous for knowing how to ring a bell at the gatehouse so as to be given food, a tradition that continues to this day (see picture 8). The trick was taught to them by the daughter of Bishop Hervey in the 1870s. The palace now has two bells – one each side of the gatehouse's window – each with a rope for the swans to pull when they are hungry.

More widely there are numerous charities across the country whose sole purpose is to rescue and protect swans and other water birds from the damage which humans accidentally, and sometimes deliberately, inflict upon them. A few of them are listed toward the back of this book.

Chapter Four

THE
MYTH

Stories about majestic swans and their magical powers have been passed down for many thousands of years across a vast array of cultures. Some date back to prehistoric times, others barely a few years. Some portray swans as passionate lovers, others as vengeful, scorned killers.

No matter the mythical meaning, these stories and beliefs often feature the contrasts and contradictions we are now familiar with. Light versus shade, shame versus grace and life versus death.

From ballets such as *Swan Lake* to fairy tales like 'The Ugly Duckling'. And from Greek myths such as 'Leda and the Swan' to urban myths like 'swans can break your arm', these tales have enhanced our appreciation of this resplendent creature.

Artwork found in Russian caves dating back as far as 18,000 BCE suggests that humans believed swans had links to death and were associated with the human soul. To this day the Buryat people of Siberia believe it's a sin to kill a swan or even to touch a feather, so sacred are these birds. When the swans arrive in springtime, these indigenous Mongolian people kneel and pray to the first one they see.

But it was the ancient Greeks who raised the swan from a vague, mysterious creature to one thought to possess the awesome power to create and destroy life and the beauty to spellbind the gods.

We have already discussed the supreme god Zeus' fascination with these magnificent birds.

But his association with them did not end with Leda. In another tale Zeus had yet another love affair, this time with the beautiful goddess Leto. She became pregnant and Zeus' wife Hera flew into a jealous rage. Fearing for her life, Leto fled to the island of Delos, where she gave birth to twins, Artemis and Apollo.

On the day Apollo was born, seven swans flew seven times around the island. The swan was thereafter sacred to Apollo, who went on to become God of the sun, arts, music and fortune-telling.

Then there is the story of how the star constellation Cygnus (Latinised Greek for 'swan') came to grace our skies. The legend tells the story of Phaethon (the child of sun god Helios) and his good friend Cycnus, who was known as a cruel and bloodthirsty man. Phaethon had long wanted the opportunity to drive his father's sun chariot. After much nagging, Helios gave permission for Phaethon to drive the chariot for one day only, but Phaethon was a terrible driver. He flew the chariot far too close to the Earth, causing rivers to dry up, deserts to form and fierce fires to break out.

Zeus soon realised he must come to the rescue. He shot the young erratic charioteer with his lighting bolt. Phaethon fell from the sky and died, landing in the River Erianus. His friend Cycnus was heartbroken. He dived into the river to retrieve the body so that a proper burial could be arranged. The devastated Cycnus sang sad songs for days on end, which Zeus found deeply moving. He allowed Cycnus to be transformed into a swan and placed him in the sky as the Cygnus star constellation. Seen in the northern hemisphere in summer or early autumn, this constellation resembles a flying swan.

Around 2,500 years ago, people began to admire the swan in mythical terms, with stories about the bird's magical powers being passed down from generation to generation.

Hundreds of years later came the Irish myth of King Lir and his children. The king and his wife Aoibh had one girl named Fionnuala, a son named Aodh and twin boys named Conn and Fiachra. One day, to the shock of the king and his children, the queen died suddenly. Following a period of mourning, the king fell in love with Aoibh's sister, Aoife. She turned out to be an evil stepmother who hated the love and attention showered upon the children by the king. One day she followed them to a nearby lake and used evil magic to transform them all into swans. The spell could not be broken until the church bells of the Monastery on Inishglora Island were rung and the children blessed by a monk. King Lir begged Aoife to break the spell, but she refused. When Aoife's father learned of his daughter's cruelty he struck her with a druid's wand, transforming her into an evil air demon forever.

The four swans spent 300 years on Lough Derravaragh, the next 300 on Irrus Domnann and the last 300 on Erris near Inishglora Island. Finally, the four swans heard the ringing of the church bells. A local monk felt sorry for them and blessed the children, whose bodies were instantly transformed back into humans. But they were now more than 900 years old, and died shortly thereafter in each other's arms. The monk buried the four children and that night he dreamed about four beautiful swans flying in the sky. At this moment he knew the four siblings were in heaven, finally reunited with their parents.

———

Running through many of the countless myths and legends about swans there is an ever-present narrative of love and a moment of uncontrolled jealousy – a trait so often seen in wild swans. The dichotomy of the swan raises its head time and again and has been developed in modern stories, most famously in Tchaikovsky's *Swan Lake*.

Modern versions of the nineteenth-century ballet have a multitude of endings, yet all remain close to the central theme of duality – grace versus violence, romance versus tragedy, good versus evil and love versus hate.

There is no hard evidence about who first wrote this story, with historians arguing over whether it stems from German or Russian fairy tales. Many believe the modern-

1. A swan on the Duke of Northumberland River, London (*www.ilikebird.uk*)

2. The classic image of two adoring swans. Home Park, London (*Sue Lindenberg*)

3. These three cygnets hatched within a few minutes of one another (*www.ilikebird.uk*)

4. An exposed swan's nest at RSPB Strumpshaw Fen, Norfolk (*www.ilikebird.uk*)

5. This cygnet went for its first swim just hours after birth (*www.ilikebird.uk*)

6. Cygnets often hop onto the back of the pen when they are tired (*Sue Lindenberg*)

7. An adult mute swan splashes down in Home Park, London (*Sue Lindenberg*)

8. Swans at Bishop's Palace in Wells ring the bell every day for food. Former operations manager George Le Roy looks on (*The Bishop's Palace*)

9. A swan's legs are designed for swimming, not walking (*Dr Ellie Rad*)

10. A cob rises up from the water after chasing away a goose (*www.ilikebird.uk*)

11. A frosty touchdown in Bushy Park, London (*Sue Lindenberg*)

12. A cob chases two Egyptian geese in Richmond Park, London (*www.ilikebird.uk*)

13. Swans sometimes hoick up a leg to regulate body temperature (*www.ilikebird.uk*)

14. Swan-snapping at Moor Green Lakes, Wokingham, Berkshire (*Matt Keel*)

15. The insides of a swan's bill are serrated to help tear plants from the riverbed (*www.ilikebird.uk*)

16. A male mute swan in Adam's Pond, Richmond Park, London
(*www.ilikebird.uk*)

17. A swan comes in to land at Home Park, London (*Sue Lindenberg*)

18. A calm dawn scene in London's Bushy Park (*Sue Lindenberg*)

day plot was actually an adaptation of a folktale called 'The Stolen Veil', written by the eighteenth-century German author Johann Karl August Musäus. Traditional takes on this classic tale begin with the heir to the throne, Prince Siegfried, preparing a ball to celebrate his 21st birthday. His mother makes clear he must use the party to choose a wife. Angry that he cannot marry for love, the young prince and his friends flee to a forest armed with a crossbow given to Siegfried by his mother. The group stumble upon a beautiful lake where he sees a flock of swans flying overhead. Keen to test his new weapon, he takes aim, but before he has time to pull the trigger, the leading swan turns into a beautiful woman called Odette.

The pair dance and Siegfried learns that Odette is a princess condemned to take the form of a swan during daylight hours after being cursed by the evil sorcerer von Rothbart, who is posing as Siegfried's mentor. This curse can only be broken by a man who pledges his heart solely to Odette. But just as the prince prepares to devote his love to her, the evil von Rothbart rips Odette from Siegfried's grasp and orders the swans to dance on the lake away from the Prince's outstretched arms. The lake is made from the tears of weeping parents whose daughters have been condemned to the same fate as Odette.

The prince returns to the celebrations at the palace and dances with each of the princesses introduced to him by his mother. Siegfried, who cannot stop thinking about

Odette, is delighted when she arrives at the ball wearing black. However, this is a trick. Von Rothbart has cast a spell on his daughter Odile, bestowing her with identical looks to the prince's true love.

Siegfried naturally whisks the beautiful woman onto the dance floor before announcing his intention to make her his wife. Just moments later he locks eyes with the real Odette, now heartbroken, who has been watching events through a window. She runs from the castle toward the lake of tears, chased by Siegfried, who by now has realised his mistake. As the pair begin another dance of love by the lake, the evil sorcerer returns once more to rip them apart.

In some versions the lovers realise they cannot break the spell. The prince's mistaken marriage announcement has condemned them to a lifetime apart. But there are other endings, most of which involve Siegfried and von Rothbart fighting on the lake before the prince rips off the sorcerer's wing and breaks the curse. These versions see von Rothbart drown and the remaining swans released from their curse, returning to their human form to live lives of happiness. In many renditions of the ballet, it is the same ballerina who plays both Odette and Odile, flicking from grace to anger, love to hate and hope to tragedy – just like a swan.

It would be hard to find a narrative which more aptly encapsulates the contrasts of the swan. Everything about it – its strength and fragility, its romance and aggression

– is all contained in one story and in some cases in one performer. Then there's its hugely complex relationship with humankind – on the one hand a friend and a lover, on the other an arch enemy with whom it fights bitterly to survive.

Similar contradictions and transformations can be found in yet another swan classic, this one written just 30 years earlier than Tchaikovsky's ballet. The contrasts in Hans Christian Andersen's fairy tale 'The Ugly Duckling' are based far more on appearance than on character.

This 1843 fable begins with a mother duck hatching a batch of eggs on a farm among other birds and animals. One of the new-born ducklings is teased and bullied by his siblings, spending much of his childhood feeling deeply unhappy. Living a life of abject loneliness and misery, he flees to the countryside and the company of wild ducks and geese. Tragically, they are all killed by hunters and he finds himself alone once more. The desperate 'ugly' duckling next finds a home with an old woman where he is once again teased, this time by her cat and hen, for his unfavourable appearance. Setting off alone once more he sees a flock of wild swans pass overhead, but being too young to fly, he cannot join them. As the winter sets in, a farmer finds him freezing in the snow and carries the exhausted bird back to his house.

Now accustomed to a life alone, the duckling is terrified of the noisy children and disappears from the farm, spending much of the winter in a cold damp cave. When springtime arrives, he spots a flock of swans descending on a nearby lake. Condemned to a life of misery unless he takes action, he decides to approach the swans, concluding it is better to be killed by these huge beautiful creatures than to live a life of ugliness and loneliness. To his amazement the swans welcome him into their group. He looks down into the water at his reflection and realises that, far from being an ugly duckling, he is in fact a beautiful swan. The flock takes to the skies.

———

These myths, fairy tales and fables are steeped in magic and mystery. Others have morphed into urban legends and modern-day beliefs about swans. It is time to separate the fact from the fiction.

Do swans sing before they die?

As I have already noted, the name 'swan' derives from the Indo-European root 'swen', meaning to sound or sing. Yet the various swan species have only ever been heard to hiss, honk or grunt. So, where does the myth come from that swans sing before they die?

Once again, its roots can be traced to Greece, with two obvious mentions of swans and singing. The Greek tragedy *Agamemnon* by Aeschylus (458 BCE) saw Helen of Troy's sister Clytemnestra compare the dead Cassandra to a swan that 'chaunts her death wail'.

Then the philosopher Plato's dialogue *Phaedo* includes a passage from Socrates spoken before he was put to death on charges of 'impiety and corruption of the young'. His last words included the passage: '... you do not think that I can see as far ahead as a swan. You know that when swans feel the approach of death, they sing – and they sing sweeter and louder on the last days of their lives because they are going back to that god whom they serve...'

But it wasn't just the Greeks who went along with this dubious belief. Many Romans believed in the 'swan song' too. Cicero declared that when a swan foresaw its death it sang 'a song of rapture'. Meanwhile, in the post-Classical world both Chaucer and Shakespeare subscribed to this belief. Chaucer included this line in the 14th-century poem *The Parliament of Fowles*:

> *The Ialous swan, ayens his deth that singeth. (The jealous swan, sings before his death).*

Shakespeare (often labelled the 'Swan of Avon') also referred to the bird's musicality in *The Merchant of Venice* (1596):

Portia: 'Let music sound while he doth
        make his choice; then, if he lose, he
        makes a swan-like end, fading in music.'

Of course, the term 'swan song' eventually came to mean the final performance or activity of a person's career, with famous performers now regularly embarking on farewell 'swan song' tours.[*]

But where and why did this myth originate? Mute swans, while not technically mute, rarely make sounds beyond the occasional hiss or grunt. The only vaguely musical noise is the soft cello-like sound of their beating wings in flight. Unless Greek mute swans commonly chose to fly during the final moments of life, we can discount mutes as the inspiration of Socrates's final moments.

What about the other species of swan? Well, the black-necked swan, like the mute, is relatively silent. The trumpeter, Bewick's and whistling swans all make a truly horrendous racket that no one would describe as a song. And the Australian black swan was not encountered by Europeans until 1697 so couldn't possibly be the source of the Greeks' inspiration.

---

[*] The most striking case involved the Australian opera singer Nellie Melba. Her swan song consisted of an eight-year-long string of 'final concerts' between 1920 and 1928. This led to the Australian phrase 'more farewells than Nellie Melba'.

That leaves the whooper swan. Known for spending wintertime in Greece, this species is perhaps the only viable candidate. The whooper traditionally makes a bizarre honking call. But the nineteenth-century Prussian zoologist and botanist Peter Pallas claims to have observed it making a 'wailing flute-like sound' as the air left its lungs for the final time. He suggested this was a by-product of its elongated tracheal loop.

Could it be that this is what Socrates heard? Could it be that it was so beautiful and memorable that he chose to speak of it with his dying breaths? Maybe – but wait. There is one final story which is included in this book for its ludicrousness rather than its logic.

Before the days when binoculars, telescopes and cameras were sold to a mass market, ornithologists had a real struggle getting up close to birds. Incredibly, many birdwatchers of the nineteenth century took to shooting them in order to get a good look.

The last ornithologist who seemed to believe swans sang before they died was the founder of the American Ornithologist Union (and bird shooter) Daniel Giraud Elliot. One sunny day on Currituck Sound, North Carolina, Elliot and a friend went on a 'bird-studying' trip (a hunting trip).

He later explained: 'A number of swans passed over us at a considerable height. We fired at them, and one splendid bird was mortally hurt. On receiving his wound, the wings became fixed and he commenced at once his song, which was continued until the water was reached, nearly half a mile away. I am perfectly familiar with every note a swan is accustomed to utter, but never before nor since have I heard any like those sung by this stricken bird. Most plaintive in character and musical tone, it sounded at times like the soft running of the notes in an octave, and as the sound was borne to us, mellowed by the distance, we stood astonished and could only exclaim, "We have heard the song of the dying swan".'

What a load of rubbish!

Do swans really sing before they die? No, they don't.

Can a swan break your arm?

Myriad works of literature exist stating that swans can break a human's arm. No real-life examples can be found. Equally, there is a huge array of printed and online material suggesting a swan, with its hollow bones, simply lacks the brute force required to break a human's thick bones. Again, there is no evidence. But I was still determined to take a stab at coming up with an answer.

Let's start by examining the makeup of a swan's wing, as this seems the only remotely feasible weapon in its arsenal capable of breaking the limb of a fully grown man (its bill is capable of a nasty peck, but would struggle to even leave a bruise). A swan's wing has around 10,000 feathers, is around 61 cm (24 in.) long and weighs around 700 g (1 lb 7 oz.). As previously mentioned, the bones are hollow to save vital weight in flight.

The flight of most waterfowl sees them flapping their wings quicker than most birds. Unlike an eagle, the bodies of waterfowl are heavy and the wings relatively small in comparison. This means there is a relatively high load on the wing and that a large amount of flapping is required for a swan to remain airborne. The swan does however have a smaller wing-load compared to other waterfowl, meaning it only beats its wings 160 times a minute compared to your average duck, which flaps at 300 times. Why is this relevant? Well, it suggests the swan generates a decent amount of power from its large, broad wings and strong chest muscles. We already know a swan's wing is capable of submerging a large struggling dog under water for more than a minute. We also know a swan's wing can keep airborne a body mass of 12.2 kg (26.8 lb) for very long periods when migrating. But strong enough to break your arm?

A force of 4,000 newtons is required to break a human femur bone (the one extending from your hip to your knee).[1] An estimated force of 3,300 newtons is required to break the average rib.[2] So let's be generous and suggest that a force of 2,000 newtons is required to break the long thin radius bone extending from the elbow to the thumb. It is after all far less protected by fat and muscle compared to the femur.

Can a swan generate that kind of force? To answer this question I carried out a string of calculations using the formula Force = Mass x Acceleration. My work was based on the speed and acceleration of a swan's wing, the weight of the wing, and the length of the wing.* The end result was that an adult swan's wing can generate a force of 79 newtons, far short of the 2,000 newtons required to break an arm. Now, as you can probably tell, I am no scientist. I have used a number of assumptions.

These are:

- That a swan's wing weighs 0.7 kg
- That the swan's wingbeat is one metre tall
- That the human arm in question is of average strength for an adult (i.e. not that of a child or an old person with a lower bone density)
- That a swan would attack a human with the same wing speed and acceleration it generates when flying
- That every single part of a swan's wing moves at the same speed.

* You can read the full calculations by visiting my website www.ilikebird.uk

Let's say I am wrong on all these assumptions; would it make a big enough difference? Even if a swan's wing weighs more, beats down faster when attacking *and* even if the swan chose to attack someone with particularly weak bones, there is simply no way these variables would bridge the gap between 79 newtons and the 2,000 required to break an arm.

Those desperate to disprove this theory may stumble across the case of a 70-year-old woman who broke her wrist after being attacked by a swan in Dublin. The *Irish Times* reported in May 2001 how the pensioner failed in a £30,000 personal injuries action against the state after being attacked by an angry cob in Phoenix Park. Mary Ryan, from Castleknock, told Dublin Circuit Civil Court: 'He knocked me to the ground. He continued to aggressively beat my legs and tried to peck me in the head.'

The article says a motorist pumping a car horn seemed to frighten the swan, giving the victim long enough to reach her vehicle. But Ms Ryan explained: 'The swan followed me and started pecking at the car and beating at it with his wings.'

Ms Ryan's case centred on the claim that there were 'no signs warning people as to the mischievous propensity and uncertain temperament of swans'. But the judge decided that neither park nor the state should assume ownership or responsibility for the actions of a swan which had merely flown in. Judge Kevin Haugh added: 'The swan, like Oliver Twist, had come back looking for more and beat her to the ground.'

It was never made clear exactly how Ms Ryan's wrist was broken in this unfortunate incident. But the judge's concluding words suggest she was knocked to the ground. I am going to stick my neck out and suggest it was almost certainly the fall which caused her injury and not the swan's wing.

Can a swan break your arm? No. In fact, I would suggest a swan is more likely to break its own wing when attacking a human.

Does the Queen own all the swans?

The first trace of people owning swans in the same way they owned land or buildings dates back to the year 966. The English King Edgar gave rights to the abbots of Croyland in Lincolnshire over stray mute swans. How these swans were marked as 'owned' is unclear. But we do know that by the twelfth century, birds' feet and bills were being clipped with small notches, with different patterns for different owners.

As we know, 1482 saw things get really interesting. The Act for Swans passed by King Edward IV declared:

> *None (but the King's son) shall have any*
> *Mark or Game of Swans of his own,*
> *or to use, except he have Lands and*
> *Tenements of Freehold worth five marks*
> *per Annum, besides Reprises; in pain to*
> *have them seised by any having lands of*
> *that value, to be divided betwixt the*
> *King and Seizor.*

From that point on, all mute swans found in the wild were marked by the royal swan master. He etched a symbol on the swans' bills or feet to denote ownership. The exact reason for this declaration has not been documented, but it was likely designed as a sweetener to strengthen relationships between the king and the influential trade guilds.

The crown took possession of the most magnificent-looking swans, while the uglier ones were divvied up between noble families, wealthy landowners and London's livery companies, such as the Vintners and the Dyers. Unmarked swans belonged to the king. Anyone caught hunting or eating a swan that was not a member of the upper class was charged with theft. (This law still exists, except if caught killing or eating swans today, you would more likely be charged with breaching wildlife conservation law, such as the Wildlife and Countryside Act 1981 which protects all wild birds.)

Tudor monarchs such as King Henry VII went a step further with a new Act in 1496 protecting the eggs of mute swans:

> *None shall take out of the nest any eggs of Falcon, Goshawk, Lanner [falcon] or Swan, in pain of a Year and a day's imprisonment, and to incur a fine at the King's pleasure, to be divided between the King and the Owner of the Ground.*

Swan ownership was rife throughout the sixteenth and seventeenth centuries with penalties for stealing them becoming ever more severe. The next 200 years saw swans continue to be bought and sold by the upper classes, particularly wealthy landowners. By the mid-nineteenth century swan stealers were even being sent to penal colonies like Australia, while others were handed sentences of hard labour lasting months on end.[3]

It was not until 1971 that parliament attempted to abolish many of the rights held by the crown over wildlife, and even then it failed to include swans. Queen Elizabeth II used her royal prerogative powers to ensure parts of the 1482 Act remained intact – chiefly the bit about royal fish and swans. Unmarked swans continued to belong to the crown.

The Wild Creatures and Forest Laws Act (1971) reads:

> *Abolition of certain rights of the Crown*
> *to wild creatures and certain related*
> *rights and franchises.*
> *There are hereby abolished —*
> *any prerogative right of Her Majesty to*
> *   wild creatures (except royal fish and*
> *   swans), together with any prerogative*
> *   right to set aside land or water for the*
> *   breeding, support or taking of wild*
> *   creatures; and*
> *any franchises of forest, free chase,*
> *   park or free warren.*

Interestingly, the Act clarified exactly which types of swans remained under the Queen's possession. Speaking in the House of Lords, the Lord Chancellor Lord Hailsham of St Marylebone explained:

> *I must make it clear that to be the*
> *object of the Royal prerogative the swan*
> *must be white, swimming in open and*
> *common rivers, and wild and unmarked.*

But what none of the legislation makes clear is that many of the mute swans on the River Thames do not belong to the crown. In fact many of them belong to a pair of trade associations. The Vintners and the Dyers are two of the many dozens of livery companies in the City of London. Each is a trade association supporting the interests of a particular industry. For example, the Worshipful Company of Vintners supports businesses involved in the import, regulation and sale of wine, while the Worshipful Company of Dyers supports various charities and businesses specialising in the development of dyeing and colouring techniques.

The two trade associations continue to hold annual 'swan-upping' ceremonies on various rivers in the south of England. At first glance these appear rather pompous affairs serving little purpose. Posh-looking people sail up and down the river in narrow canoes catching visibly distressed swans before 'upping' the birds with the companies' individual marks. There is, however, a greater good. The ceremonies – held in late July when swans are largely flightless due to their moulting feathers – see 'uppers' record how many birds they find while checking for signs of disease or injury. The information they collate is sent to the British Trust for Ornithology to help with conservation efforts.

The events, held in Middlesex, Surrey, Buckinghamshire, Berkshire and Oxfordshire, are directed by the Queen's official swan marker. Swans caught by Queen's 'uppers' are left unmarked except for a lightweight ring linked to the BTO's database.

Those caught by the Dyers and Vintners receive a different ring on the opposite leg. In the past, rather than being ringed, swans' bills would be nicked using a metal instrument. As for all the country's other unmarked swans, they belong to the Queen thanks to King Edward IV's 1482 Act.*

But how and when have these various pieces of legislation been tested? The most striking case involved none other than the Master of the Queen's Music, who at the time was Sir Peter Maxwell Davies. In the spring of 2005 Sir Peter found the carcass of a migrating whooper swan near his home on the island of Sanday in the Scottish Orkneys. The poor swan had apparently flown into a set of power lines. According to the *Guardian*, Sir Peter called the Royal Society for the Protection of Birds (RPSB), which advised him to dispose of the bird. Instead, he left the corpse to mature outside his cottage, softening up the meat to make some tasty terrine. He told the newspaper: 'I was under the illusion it would be all right to eat the best parts, rather than feed them to the cat. I was going to use the breast and leg meat. I've done it before and it really is delicious… the meat is very dark and rich. It's a bit like pheasant with a hint of venison as well.'

Unluckily for him, while he was away on business, patrolling officers spotted the dead body hanging outside his home. They returned with a search warrant under the

---

* There is a process by which individuals can apply for a licence to own mute swans, but it is long, deliberately bureaucratic and very few people can be bothered.

aforementioned Wildlife and Countryside Act 1981, and confiscated the body.

The then 70-year-old explained: 'They took a pair of swan's wings they found in a shed (from previous discoveries). I was going to give them to the Sanday school for their nativity play. Those they have already got are looking a bit dusty, and these would have been ideal for the angel Gabriel.'

Sir Peter escaped with a caution. He told BBC News he would have considered prison a 'new experience' at his age, before adding: 'Being Master of the Queen's Music, I might have to do porridge with a ball and chain in the Tower of London.'

Levity aside, this case is interesting for a number of reasons. Firstly, we can only assume the Northern Constabulary suspected Sir Peter had killed the protected swan, as otherwise there would have been no reason to seek a warrant. But this is highly unlikely to have been the case, as Sir Peter was a keen environmentalist and RSPB supporter.

Secondly, this case occurred in Scotland, a land where King Edward IV's 1482 Act does not apply. Furthermore, the bird was not a mute swan and so the law is irrelevant.

But were 'terrine-gate' to have occurred in England or Wales, and involved a mute rather than a whooper, it would have been interesting to observe whether law enforcers used the Wildlife and Countryside Act 1981 – based on conservation – or the King Edward IV Act 1482

– based on ownership. I can find only one case which appears to meet the criteria.

In March 2014 a man was convicted and fined £110 after killing a swan in Hildenborough, Kent. The 46-year-old was photographed by a fisherman beheading the adult cob and stuffing it in his rucksack.

Police traced the man, originally from Turkey, to his house in Tonbridge and found the bird chopped into pieces and neatly stored in his freezer. The man told the *Evening Standard*: 'I did not know what type of bird it was. I didn't know the Queen owned them. I like the Queen very much. The moment the police told me what I did was wrong, I said I was sorry.'

While his comments about Her Majesty are touching, they are somewhat irrelevant to this case as he was charged under the Wildlife and Countryside Act 1981. It seems that the law enforcers of today have long moved away from using King Edward's out-of-date law and now quite rightly focus on conserving the great British countryside, rather than the Queen's possessions. But the law is the law and until someone changes it...

Does the Queen own all the swans? No. Not all of them. The swans on the River Thames are divided between the Crown, the Vintners' Company and the Dyers' Company. All unmarked mutes found elsewhere do however belong to Her Majesty.

Do swans mate for life?

Discussions around swans and love are often based around the belief that they mate for life, forever faithful to one partner until the day they die.

Writers have built upon this myth with tales and fables. In Shakespeare's *As You Like It*, Celia talks of her relationship with Rosalind in the following terms:

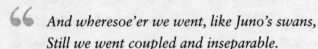

> *And wheresoe'er we went, like Juno's swans,*
> *Still we went coupled and inseparable.*

While there is some merit to the notion of swan pairs being 'inseparable', the full truth is slightly more complicated. Swans are doubtless more faithful to partners than most other birds. Recent studies put the monogamy rate at around 85 per cent.[4] (The same is true for turkeys, vultures, puffins and bald eagles.) This is extremely high for birds and very impressive compared to humans in the western world, where some estimates for monogamy rates in marriage are around 40 per cent for men and 65 for women.[5] But researchers have observed plenty of cobs straying from nesting sites to seek out female attention elsewhere. Pairings who have had one or more unsuccessful broods are also more likely to go their separate ways.

It is quite undeniable, however, that in the world of the mute swan, the cob and the pen's relationship extends far beyond mating and breeding. The pair stay together outside the breeding season and appear to enjoy one another's company. There is also plenty of evidence suggesting swans mourn a mate's passing. Many never find love again, spending the rest of their days making little or no effort to find a new partner. Widowed females have even been known to build a nest and brood thin air for up to six weeks and, of course, I have first-hand experience of a cob circling the lifeless body of its deceased partner.

But possibly the most endearing examples of devotion involve swans in rescue centres. Rescue workers have observed that swans recover from injuries and operations more quickly when joined by their partner or kin.[6] Aristotle suggested that swans were humans in an ideal form: cute babies; loving parents who mate for life; loyal, protective, gentle fathers. It would seem that swans are not only sociable creatures but capable of genuine love, or at least that's what I like to believe.

Do swans mate for life? Yes, just not all of them. Most stay together and continue mating and nurturing young cygnets until one of them passes away.

Do posh people eat swans?

Mute swans are entwined with wealth and nobility in all kinds of ways. The Queen owns most of the swans in the United Kingdom, while history shows that swan purchasing, swan selling and swan eating were pursuits of the rich for many hundreds of years. But to what extent is this still true? Do posh people continue to eat swans to this day?

We have already touched on two different theories as to when people living in Britain first encountered and hunted swans. The first postulates that humankind started killing and eating swans around 900,000 years ago when an early human species, *Homo antecessor*, is first thought to have lived in what we now call the British Isles. It is unlikely that they would have passed up the opportunity to kill and eat such a large, slow and rewarding meal. Back then the birds would have been clubbed or grabbed with bare hands, although much more recently it's possible that our own species, *Homo sapiens*, would have been using basic blunt wooden arrows by around 1900 BCE, shortly after the completion of Stonehenge.

The second theory, as we have already seen, involves Richard I (Richard the Lionheart) and claims that he celebrated his Cypriot triumph by putting swans on the Thames.[7]

Of course, it is perfectly plausible that both are correct – with a gap somewhere in the middle where mute swans were wiped out by disease. But there is no evidence to suggest this was the case. What we do know for certain is that 'swanherds', people who tend to swans, existed as far back as the 1040s. The Abbotsbury Swannery near

Dorset's Chesil Beach was set up to raise cygnets to be served at feasts. (It's now a quaint tourist attraction which cares for swans.) This seems to put the Lionheart theory firmly to bed, or at least to suggest King Richard was only responsible for introducing the swans on the Thames.

But Richard I was not the only king with a penchant for swans. Henry III requested 40 of the birds be served at his Christmas feast in 1247. In 1251 he went even further, asking for 125 to be transported down from Northumberland to his holiday home in Lincoln.[8] By 1274 the price of a swan was three shillings compared to five pence for a goose and four pence for a pheasant.[9] In today's money that would be £109.47 for a swan, £15.20 for a goose and £12.16 for a pheasant.

Bird price conversions[10]

Bird for sale	Price in 1274	Worth in wages (skilled tradesman) in 1274	Value in today's money
Swan	Three shillings	15 days	£109.47
Goose	Five pence	3 days	£15.20
Pheasant	Four pence	1.5 days	£12.16

Over the next two centuries, swans were typically roasted and served up whole, usually after being fattened up with barley, maize and malt. It was found that the birds fed much more readily in groups than when isolated in pens. But chefs had to be careful when choosing a swan. Too young and there was barely any meat; too old and it tasted of fishy mutton. A large cygnet, possibly two or three years old, seemed the order of the day.

A recipe found in 1439 said:

> *Take gizzards, and livers, and heart of Swan; and if the guts are fatty, slit them, clean them, and cast them there to, and boil them in fair water; and then take them up, and hew them small, and then cast them into the same broth, (but strain it through a strainer first); and cast thereto powdered pepper, cinnamon, and vinegar, and salt, and let boil.*
>
> *And then take the blood of the Swan, and fresh broth, and bread, and draw them through a strainer, and cast thereto; and let boil together.*
>
> *And then take powder of ginger, when it is almost enough, & put thereto, and serve forth with the Swan.*[11]

Another, found in a fifteenth-century manuscript, explained:

> *Cut a swan in the roof of the mouth*
> *toward the brain end-long, and let him*
> *bleed, and keep the blood for entrails;*
> *or else knit a knot in his neck.*
> *And so let his neck break; then*
> *scald him.*
> *Draw him and roast him even as thou*
> *do goose in all points, and serve him*
> *forth with entrails.*[12]

The truth is that during these times it was the rich who owned swans, who sold swans, who bought swans and who ate swans. As we know, the meat became yet more exclusive when a law was passed in 1482 banning anyone except royalty and nobility from owning them. They graced the tables of kings and were exchanged as gifts between wealthy landowners. So contrary to popular belief, swans were never illegal to eat – just illegal for poor people to eat.

By around the mid-1600s, potted swan was beginning to overtake roast swan as the most popular style of preparing the bird. The cooking technique was popular among the upper classes, and by 1739 the cookery-book writer Eliza Smith had mastered the art:

> *Bone and skin your Swan, and beat the flesh in a mortar, taking out the strings as you beat it; then take some clear fat bacon, and beat with the Swan, and when 'tis of a light flesh-colour, there is bacon enough in it;*
>
> *And when 'tis beaten till 'tis like dough, 'tis enough; then season it with pepper, salt, cloves, mace, and nutmeg, all beaten fine; mix it well with your flesh, and give it a beat or two all together; then put it in an earthen pot, with a little claret and fair water, and at the top two pounds of fresh butter spread over it; cover it with coarse paste, and bake it with bread;*
>
> *Then turn it out into a dish, and squeeze it gently to get out the moisture; then put it in a pot fit for it; and when 'tis cold, cover it over with clarified butter, and next day paper it up. In this manner you may do Goose, Duck, or Beef, or Hare's flesh.*[13]

A century later and the recipes were no more enticing. A deeply unappealing cooking technique from an 1870 book was designed to help Victorian housewives. It advised fattening up cygnets from birth, ready for consumption as adolescents. The book's compiler, Ross Murray, told readers:

> *The cygnets when all hatched are of a slaty-grey, which grows lighter as they grow older. The cygnets of the wild swan are white. But it is of the grey cygnets we have to speak.*
>
> *They are hatched in June. If it is intended to eat them, they must be taken from their parents and put into a separate swan pond, at the end of August or first week in September.*
>
> *After they have been 'hopped or upped', as it is called, from their native place grass is thrown to them twice a day with their other food for a fortnight.*
>
> *They are fattened on barley: a coomb each cygnet suffices for the fattening.*
>
> *The corn is set in shallow tubs just under water.*
>
> *Cygnets can only be fattened before the white feathers appear; after that no feeding will do any good; as soon as*

a white feather shows they will cease
fattening, no matter what food they have.
They can consequently only be eaten
in December, and they are a capital and
magnificent Christmas dish.
Their weight then will be from 25 lbs
to 28 lbs.[14]

He recommends serving the dish with four miniature swans carved from turnips, and ends with one of his favourite poems to explain how the bird should be prepared (written in Norfolk in 1843 – author unknown):

To roast a swan:
Take three pounds of beef, beat fine in a mortar,
Put it into a Swan—that is, when you've caught her;
Some pepper, sauce, mace, some nutmeg, and onion,
Will heighten the flavour in gourmand's opinion.
Then tie it up tight with a small piece of tape,
That the gravy and other things may not escape.
A meal paste, rather stiff, should be laid on the breast,
And some whited brown paper could cover the rest.
Fifteen minutes at least ere the Swan you take down,
Pull the paste off the bird that the breast may get
brown.

And we mustn't forget…

The Gravy:

To gravy of beef, good and strong, I opine,
You'll be right if you add half a pint of port wine;
Pour this through the Swan—yes, quite through the
belly,
Then serve the whole up with some hot currant-jelly.[15]

It appears however there was a whole host of other ways for posh people to serve swan. After the future prime minister, Benjamin Disraeli, had met new MP William Gladstone at the Lord Chancellor's Dinner in 1835, he is said to have told his sister: 'we had a swan very white and tender, and stuffed with truffles, the best company there.'

We know that as late as 1974 swans were still being eaten in the UK, but in very few places – possibly only one. The 'feast of the cygnets' was a distinctly pompous annual affair in the City of London's Vintners' Hall. The cooked bird was presented on a silver platter during an opulent procession to the sound of trumpets before a carefully chosen singer of the time belted out a rendition of a song entitled, unsurprisingly, 'The Swan'.[16]

It seems the Vintners' Company has long ceased gorging on swans. Its website now explains:

 The Swan Feast takes place every year.
Cooked like a turkey or a chicken, swans

> *were a medieval delicacy – 'stuffed*
> *with herbs and pork fat, sealed in a*
> *paste of flour and water and roasted*
> *for 2–3 hours until tender'. The annual*
> *Swan Feast held on the last Thursday*
> *of November maintains this tradition.*
> *However, swan as a culinary delight has*
> *not lived up to its medieval reputation –*
> *the muscly legs and wings are very tough*
> *meat, and the birds are no longer eaten.*

So is there anyone in the UK who still eats swan?

The short answer is no. The 1482 act banned anyone except royalty and nobility from owning and killing (and therefore eating) swans. It is now the case that swan ownership is divided between two trade associations (whose members no longer eat swans or sell swans) and the Queen. There is no evidence that she trades swans or that the meat tickles her taste buds.

In America the hunting of swans is still relatively easy for those with the correct licence – but crucially the swans are almost never eaten. There are sporadic reports of swans being killed and eaten but certainly not en masse.

Upon discussing this topic with friends and family, I found their reaction to the thought of eating swan meat was one of revulsion. The most common comments were:

'How could you eat something so beautiful?'

'Swans have a human-like quality, which would make them more difficult to eat.'

'It would taste disgusting.'

'It wouldn't fit in the oven.'

Of course, some of these points are vaguely, maybe even acutely, hypocritical. Should we only eat ugly animals? Are pheasants and deer not beautiful? Is a lamb not more adorable than a swan?

The second comment may have more merit. Few of us have the same regular close contact with a chicken, pig, cow or lamb that we do with a swan. Few of us regularly feed a pig roots and berries in the same way we feed a swan bread. We therefore fail to notice the human personality and emotional traits in those animals – such as anger, fear or love for family. It is also true that humankind over the years has tended to eat animals which are (or are at least seem to be) less intelligent and therefore less like humans.

I believe people in the UK divide animals into four categories of edibility, illustrated below. These are:

a) **Never**: those we adore (pets):
- Dogs
- Cats

b) **Extremely unlikely**: those we admire (which mostly tend to be beautiful and/or are deemed to be intelligent and/or possessing human-like qualities):

- Dolphins
- Swans
- Horses
- Monkeys
- Puffins

c) **Sometimes frowned upon:** those we eat, but less often. These tend to be less beautiful and often striking in appearance:
  - Snails
  - Rabbits
  - Deer
  - Pigeons
  - Buffalo
  - Pheasants
  - Geese
  - Kangaroo
  - Alligators
  - Crocodile
  - Frogs
  - Ostrich

d) **Common:** those we eat in huge quantities (not attractive, not human-like, not particularly intelligent, rarely wild and very tasty). The lamb is maybe an exception (they are cute and eaten in huge quantities):
  - Chickens
  - Turkeys
  - Cows

- Sheep
- Most fish

Some of the animals in the second group are perfectly pleasant to eat. I would never gorge on a critically endangered puffin but I have tasted horse in Serbia and found it very palatable. I am told dolphin tastes like beef liver – far easier to eat than more commonly snacked-upon animals such as snails and frogs.

Of course, like many others, I'm a complete hypocrite when it comes to eating meat. I have not tasted swan – largely because the Queen owns most of them and declines to sell them to her citizens. Even if I could, I would find it difficult. I too have fallen into the trap of treating some wild animals – such as geese and ducks – as 'food' when it suits me, but scoff at the idea of eating swans. Swans have shown beauty, intelligence and personality in their interactions with me. I've therefore unconsciously placed a higher moral value on their lives. There is no evidence a swan is significantly more intelligent than a duck, yet we as a society have grown to love swans rather than eat them.

Do posh people eat swans? They used to, but not anymore. The Queen, the Vintners Company and the Dyers Company own most, if not all the swans. They do not eat them, nor sell them to others to eat.

Are immigrants killing and eating swans?

Swans were thrust into the limelight in quite spectacular fashion in November 2012, when Lord Leveson published the long-awaited findings of his inquiry into the culture, practices and ethics of the British press.

One of the most explosive criticisms of the tabloid media centred around a story by *The Sun* which featured the headline 'Swan Bake'. The article alleged that gangs of eastern European asylum seekers were killing and eating swans from London's ponds and lakes. Unidentified people were cited as witnesses to the phenomenon.

The inquiry concluded there was 'no basis to the story' and stressed that *The Sun* was 'unable to defend the article' against a Press Complaints Commission case.

Another story, by *The Daily Star*, was topped with the headline 'Asylum seekers eat our donkeys'. Eastern Europeans were this time joined by Somalians as the wrongly accused culprits in a tabloid investigation into the disappearance of nine donkeys in Greenwich Royal Park. Of this story, Leveson said:

> *Police were reported as having no idea what had happened to the donkeys but, in a piece of total speculation, the story went on to claim that donkey meat was a speciality in Somalia and Eastern Europe, that there were 'large numbers of Somalian*

> *asylum-seekers' in the area and some Albanians nearby, and concluded that asylum seekers had eaten the donkeys.*

After highlighting these examples, Lord Leveson concluded:

> *It is one thing for a newspaper to take the view that immigration should be reduced, or that the asylum and/or human rights system should be reformed, and to report on true stories which support those political views. It is another thing to misreport stories either wilfully or reckless as to their truth or accuracy, in order to ensure that they support those political views. And it does appear that certain parts of the press do, on occasion, prioritise the political stance of the title over the accuracy of the story.*

Of course, as we have already seen, recent immigrants can sometimes have a different cultural understanding of what is acceptable to eat – that would be true in any culture. But from isolated incidents like the man who cut up a swan and put it in his freezer, it's all too easy and all too common for the press to whip up a maelstrom of suspicion and outrage based on little but hearsay and tittle-tattle.

A quick scan of the internet shows these articles were not alone in pointing the finger at immigrants for the abuse of British animals, with swans often front and centre.

A *Daily Mail* article in August 2007 claimed swans on Leighton Buzzard's Grand Union Canal were regularly being chased by a gang of 'hungry, knife-wielding Eastern Europeans'. The piece said Polish and Lithuanian immigrants had been spotted 'dragging the 20 lb birds away' with swan carcasses found butchered on the towpath.

Another *Daily Mail* article, this time in March 2010, was headlined: 'Slaughter of the swans: As carcasses pile up and migrant camps are built on river banks, Peterborough residents are too frightened to visit the park.'

And in June 2008, the *Star* once more took a pot shot at immigrants under the banner 'Poles in a flap over don't-eat-swan sign'. The story, again without sources, claimed there was a furious backlash from Poles after signs depicting a swan flanked by a knife and fork with a red line across it were put up near a lake in Newark, Nottinghamshire. The paper contacted the Polish Embassy for comment after alleging several swans had gone missing following an influx of Polish nationals. The perplexed Polish spokesperson simply said: 'I don't know where this information comes from. It doesn't happen.'

The Met Police were finally forced to release a statement after more tabloid reports claimed a 'major investigation' had been launched after an 'official Metropolitan Police report' blamed 'Eastern European gangs' for a spate of swan deaths. The Scotland Yard spokesperson said: 'There is no police report. There appears to be a perception that this may be attributable to Eastern Europeans. We stress we have no evidence of this.'

> Do eastern European immigrants kill and eat swans? I am sure that someone has, once upon a time, but no, as a matter of course they don't.

If a swan has an orange-stained head, does that mean it has been attacked by vandals?

While most adult swans possess the clean white finish we're familiar with, you may notice that some have a rusty orange stain to their heads. Many people fear the swan has been attacked with paint or other substances. Fear not. Many of our rivers are naturally iron-rich, and this is what has tinted the head a dirty orange colour as the swan dips it into the water to feed.

> Have swans with orange-stained heads been attacked by vandals? Almost certainly not.

Do swans with lumps under their bills have 'bird' cancer?

From time to time you may see a swan with a bushy-looking ball under its bill. This can often look sinister, much like a deformity or a cancerous growth. Well, you can relax: it is almost certainly a grass ball which has gathered there while the swan was feeding. While irritating, it is unlikely to cause too much harm. If you are in any doubt, the Swan Sanctuary invites people to call them and discuss their concerns (see further information at the back of this book).

> **Do swans with lumps under their bills have 'bird' cancer? Almost certainly not. It is more likely to be a grass ball which has gathered while feeding.**

Do swans swim with their leg up when injured?

If I had a pound for every time someone told me a swan can break your arm, I would be a very rich man. If I had a pound for every time someone told me they had seen a swan with an injured leg, I'd be less rich, but still better off than now. It's an easy mistake to make. As a child I too saw countless swans swimming on lakes and rivers with a leg awkwardly hoicked up onto their backs rather than pedalling the water beneath them. I also pondered whether I should call the RSPCA. It took years to discover this is something swans do to regulate their body temperature (see picture 13).

The feet are two of the few swan body parts not covered by feathers, meaning blood vessels are in closer contact with the air. The swan's large feet and their wide surface area mean they are great at absorbing heat from the air if the water is too cold, or releasing heat from the body to the air if the water is too hot. So hoicking a leg helps swans to remain a comfortable temperature all year round.

> **Do swans swim with their leg up when injured? No, they don't. Breathe a sigh of relief and tell all your friends!**

Is it bad to feed swans bread?

Humans have been supplementing the diets of swans, geese and ducks with bread for centuries. The ritual allows us to interact with nature at close quarters, with a food that most of us have knocking around in the kitchen. But are we doing more harm than good?

You don't need a post-grad in biology to work out that bread offers very little nutritional value to a bird. In humans, bread acts as a satisfying answer to hunger pangs. In swans it is much the same, but could do more damage.

Studies over the last two decades suggest bread could be one of the main causes of 'angel wing', a condition most commonly found among ducks and geese, but thought to affect swans too. Birds gorge on dough for years on end in the lakes and rivers of our towns and cities. As a result, some begin to develop a peculiar growth on their wing which hinders their flight. The deformity means they are more vulnerable to predation but, more worrying still, they pass on the nutritional imbalance to their offspring, which develop the same condition.

Wildfowl & Wetlands Trust animal health officer Martin Brown spoke to me in October 2015 for an article I was writing for *Birdwatching Magazine*. He said: 'It would be better to give them seeds or specially made 'fat balls' which are sold in pet shops and WWT Wetland Centre shops. These have a mixture of nutrients and protein as well as the fat that birds need to survive the winter.'

Bread has been found to leave birds bloated and lethargic and, in some cases, simply too lazy to forage for more nutritional foods. The repercussions for the surrounding eco-system can be damaging. Mouldy bread sinks to the bottom of our waterways, attracting a plethora of algae. Much of this is poisonous to fish and possibly deadly to any predators which feed on them. Furthermore, rotting bread attracts rats, which can attack cygnets.

It is sad that in this particular instance, human intentions that are good and pure lead to a bad and unintended outcome. Of course, bread in small quantities is not a problem. But once every tourist, hiker and dog walker has thrown in a small quantity, it quickly turns into a huge amount.

Is it bad to feed swans bread? Not in small quantities, but too much is a problem. Better to feed them wheat, maize, lettuce, watercress or cabbage. And don't worry about overfeeding a swan the good stuff. Unlike some animals, they simply stop eating when they are full. But make sure to throw your healthy swan food into the water, as enticing swans onto land brings them closer to dangers such as dogs and cars.

Chapter Five

THE
AVIATOR

A swan in flight is a truly spectacular sight. Yet there are few poems, paintings or scripts that depict what, for me, is its most exciting quality: its majesty in the sky. Maybe Michelangelo never saw a swan run on water before slowly launching itself into the air. Perhaps Socrates never witnessed a swan gliding smoothly above a lake before skimming gently down to earth. Did Cicero never hear the cello-like beat of wings before looking up to see a magnificent flying-V?

Greeks, Romans, Normans and writers from countless other peoples described the swan's majesty, its grace and its standing as a symbol of love. But nearly every case saw the swan swimming on water or nestled in the passionate embrace of a beautiful woman – rarely flying.

The Irish poet W. B. Yeats certainly had a bash in 1916, but even his attempts at describing the swan's flight seem like an afterthought, referring to its 'clamorous' wings and the 'bell-beat' of its wing strokes.

The Wild Swans at Coole

The trees are in their autumn beauty,
The woodland paths are dry,
Under the October twilight the water
Mirrors a still sky;
Upon the brimming water among the stones
Are nine-and-fifty swans.

The nineteenth autumn has come upon me
Since I first made my count;
I saw, before I had well finished,
All suddenly mount
And scatter wheeling in great broken rings
Upon their clamorous wings.
I have looked upon those brilliant creatures,
And now my heart is sore.
All's changed since I, hearing at twilight,
The first time on this shore,
The bell-beat of their wings above my head,
Trod with a lighter tread.
Unwearied still, lover by lover,
They paddle in the cold
Companionable streams or climb the air;
Their hearts have not grown old;
Passion or conquest, wander where they will,
Attend upon them still.
But now they drift on the still water,
Mysterious, beautiful;
Among what rushes will they build,
By what lake's edge or pool
Delight men's eyes when I awake some day
To find they have flown away?

John Dryden's couplet in his translation of Virgil's
The Aeneid is perhaps more fitting:

> *Like a long team of snowy swans on high,*
>   *Which clap their wings and cleave the*
> *liquid sky.*

Of course, it's fair to say the swan is not among the world's greatest flyers. Poets, playwrights and authors are quite rightly drawn to the soaring of an eagle, the stoop of a peregrine or the speed of a swift. But can you name a bird which matches the swan for drama on take-off or suspense as it glides down to the cool water? Maybe we have come to take it for granted. It is semi-domesticated, after all, so perhaps we have been spoiled with too much access. Not me.

But it's no coincidence that the swan has been compared to one of the most beautiful aircraft ever made – Concorde. Sadly, now absent from our skies, this incredible feat of engineering dominated aviation headlines from 1976 to 2003, when the last one was taken out of service.

Stewardess Sally Armstrong worked on it for seven years. In her book *Vintage Champagne on the Edge of Space* she describes it as 'a glamorous icon', and a 'favourite with A-listers, politicians, and royalty'. She says the aircraft was a symbol 'to be proud of' and talks of how people's 'eyes lit up' at seeing it pass overhead. Sound familiar?

Immediately recognisable for its graceful shape, smooth lines and tremendous noise, this magnificent machine had a long, white neck, thinning towards the nape. Its white torso was beautifully sleek, the wheels neatly tucked away. Splendid and regal when airborne, it looked somewhat ordinary when taxiing on land.

As with the Vintners' 'feast of the cygnets', its exclusive clientele was served food on silver platters, and – just like the swan – it flew at enormous altitudes to avoid turbulence. It was also largely associated with society's elite and was a huge favourite with the royals. It was for some time one of our most iconic symbols. Concorde, like the swan, represented not just quality, but Britain at its best.

Wings of a swan

When it comes to flight, both Concorde and the swan have a graceful exterior which hides a surprisingly light frame designed to minimise weight. Like many heavy flying birds, the bones of a swan resemble a semi-solid 'honeycomb', meaning they are light, agile but also weak.

As for the rest of the body, large parts of it are designed for swimming, not flying, and certainly not for walking. The bird's underside has even been used as a blueprint for boat designers. The breadth of the torso tapers off towards the rear like a ship's stern. The huge webbed feet beneath two short legs make excellent paddles, propelling it through water faster than most water birds. But what makes swans such excellent swimmers also makes them comical walkers. The bulky frame is hard to control on land, the legs too short and too far from the centre of gravity. It is this which gives the swan that embarrassing waddle they exhibit on land (see picture 9).

But while its land movement can be a cause for ridicule, its movement through the air cannot. The French ophthalmologist André Rochon-Duvigneaud famously wrote that 'a bird is a wing guided by an eye'. This is certainly true of the swan. We already know its eyes are designed to act as a radar, scanning for predators through almost 360 degrees. With such a panoramic view of the world they are able to guide those giant wings down onto our lakes and rivers and, in most cases, away from danger. But how do the wings work and how do they help swans look so stunning in flight?

A swan's wing contains 11 large primary feathers, attached to the wingtip. These quills drive the bird through the air. The downward stroke of the wingbeat means the fingers of the feathers separate, allowing each primary feather to twist like a propeller.[1] The wing itself is moved by impressive breast muscles pumping regularly at around 160 flaps per minute, stopping only rarely for glides. The wingtips move faster than the rest of the wing, forming a figure-of-eight pattern through the air.

Swans fly at around 30 mph but are able to slow to 18 mph without stalling and falling from the sky. They max out at 50 mph. But dragging 12 kg (26.5 lb) of weight through the air at 30 mph is tiring work. Some scientists suggest the ratio of mass to wing size puts the bird on the cusp of being rendered flightless.[2] So what other tricks do they deploy to make flying less demanding? And how have humans copied these tactics?

Ducks, geese and swans are among the select families of birds which save energy by flying in V-formations. The wings of flying birds leave mini vortices in their wake. It is these whirling masses of fluid air that can be used as lift by anything flying behind them, though only at the correct distance and angle. Too close or too far and the birds will find themselves flying in turbulent air – a very uncomfortable experience.[*] Of course, the bird leading the pack benefits from none of this science, but that's where ducks, geese and swans are particularly clever. By taking it in turns at the front of the formation, they share the load, ensuring each swan puts in a shift, followed by a rest. It's a tactic which has been used by humans in all kinds of activities.

Squadrons of military aircraft fly in Vs or echelons (half Vs) to ensure that, collectively, they burn off less fuel and can therefore fly further. This could be the difference between reaching the bombing target and returning home, or completing the mission but crashing into the sea on the way back.

---

[*] Remember how 'Maverick' flew through 'Ice Man's' jet wash in *Top Gun*?

Professional cycling also uses teams that work together as a single unit to preserve energy. In the annual Tour de France the 'team leader' rarely cycles to the front as he needs to conserve his energy. His teammates rotate to work on his behalf, shielding him from the wind and the turbulent air. In Formula One motor racing, some engineers forge entire careers around spotting and capitalising on aerodynamic marginal gains to give their car the edge on race day.

For the swan and the cyclist, the concept is based on the need to conserve the body's energy. For the military and the racing car it is about conserving the same thing in the form of fuel. So why has the civil aviation industry not done something similar? Would this not save them millions of pounds in fuel? Well, some companies *are* considering it.

Fuel costs, the 2008/09 financial crisis and the coronavirus pandemic have put a huge strain on the balance sheets of airlines and aircraft manufacturers in recent years. According to an article in the *Economist* magazine in 2019, aeronautical engineers at firms such as Airbus have been tasked with finding ways to shave 10 per cent off the fuel consumption of the aircraft they produce.

Researchers have been looking at commercial airliners flying together in groups, like military squadrons, investigating the effects of different design modifications, loading the planes with ballast to replicate the weight of passengers. The plane flying in front deploys smoke so that the pilot behind can see exactly where the vortices are produced. Part of the vortex contains a helpful updraft while another part features a turbulent downdraft. The trailing pilots gradually move closer while scientists in the back of the plane interrogate the data to find the 'sweet spot', the distance and angle that give maximum lift without spilling the drinks of the imaginary passengers. More lift means pilots can reduce the power, meaning less fuel is burned.

The biggest hurdle of all will be satisfying air-traffic controllers and regulators that flying squadrons of commercial aircraft is safe. After all, at cruising speed a plane can cover two or three kilometres in just a few seconds, giving trailing aircraft very little time to take evasive action if something happens in front. And how will passengers feel? Competition between airlines means frequent flyers have become accustomed to a choice of flight times spread evenly throughout the day. This may change if airlines work together and take off in formations to save fuel.[3]

If safety concerns can be allayed, however, there will be a huge fan base among green campaigners. Less fuel means less carbon dioxide in the atmosphere, which helps slow the rate of climate change. And so it becomes clear that swans have not just inspired some of our greatest art and literature, but some of our science as well.

Disaster strikes

Despite offering so much inspiration to human aviation, swans and geese have on occasion brought these designs crashing back down to earth. Large waterfowl are not particularly agile in the air and are often unable to avoid large aircraft flying at tremendous speeds. The impact can be catastrophic.

Birds have been causing problems for aircraft since the very early days of flight. The first known bird strike with an aircraft occurred in 1908. The first fatality happened in 1912 when a gull became entangled in the control wires of a Wright Flyer, causing the plane to crash and the pilot to die.

Unsurprisingly, as aircraft became faster, the damage caused by bird strikes became more severe. Windscreens were smashed, cabins depressurised, fuel tanks punctured, wings damaged and engines destroyed. And needless to say, the bigger the bird, the bigger the impact – and swans and geese are pretty big. By far the most famous example in recent years is the story of Flight 1549, recently made into the hit movie *Sully*, featuring Tom Hanks.

On 15 January 2009, a US Airways flight carrying 150 passengers took off from New York City's LaGuardia Airport for what should have been a short flight to Charlotte, North Carolina. Just minutes later the Airbus A320, piloted by Captain Chesley B. 'Sully' Sullenberger III, collided with a flock of Canada geese.

The impact destroyed both engines, killing the geese (Sully remembers smelling burnt chicken as the geese passed through the two turbine engines), leaving the pilot with no option but to glide the aircraft down to an emergency landing on the Hudson River.

Miraculously, everyone on board survived. This was largely thanks to Sully's skilful flying and the speedy response from boat crews, who rescued passengers stranded on the aircraft's wings just before it sank into the icy-cold water.

Many incidents do not end so well. The deadliest incident involving swans occurred in the skies near Baltimore, USA, in 1962. A Vickers 745D Viscount operated by United Airlines was travelling from New York (Newark) airport to Washington DC when it struck a flock of whistling swans. The impact damaged the aircraft's tail elevators so badly that it dropped into a nosedive before crashing in Ellicott City, killing all 17 people on board. Manufacturing regulations were later altered to ensure tails could withstand the impact of a bird strike.

The worst incident involving any bird also occurred in America, this time in Boston in 1960. A Lockheed Electra aircraft was travelling from New York City's LaGuardia Airport to Philadelphia, Pennsylvania, when it hit a flock of starlings six seconds after take-off. The birds were sucked into three of the four engines causing catastrophic damage. The aircraft's nose pitched up as it crashed into Winthrop Bay. Only ten of the 72 people on board survived.

According to the UK's Civil Aviation Authority (CAA) there are around 1,500 bird strikes every year. Species range from black-headed gulls to budgerigars. Of course, very few swans die from collisions with planes compared to collisions with cars, and swans should be far more concerned about the steps humans are taking to avoid an airborne collision than the collision itself. That's because humans now go to monumental lengths to protect pilots, passengers and aircraft from this danger. These measures involve shooting birds which fly near airport flightpaths, or destroying nests. But increasingly the most effective methods are rooted in the 'management' of habitat.

The military and the Civil Aviation Authority work alongside local and central government to ensure airfields and the surrounding land do not include features such as rubbish dumps or landfill sites which could attract crows and kites. Long grass is also avoided to ensure skylarks are discouraged from nesting. Other airfields have introduced regular flare launches to scare birds away while some use laser beams. Smaller airports have even sent staff out shaking rattles to scare off any birds.[4] The management of land, with the specific aim of making it unattractive to birds, is bad news for swans and bad news for birds in general. Far more will suffer or perish from the destruction of suitable habitat than they will from collisions with aircraft.

Short-haul migration

Concorde is now sadly grounded, with one of the aircraft displayed outside a hangar at London's Heathrow airport. The terror attacks on 9/11, coupled with the fatal Concorde disaster near Paris in July 2000, saw demand for the swan of the aviation world decline. British Airways and Air France retired their fleets in 2003. It was a sad end for such an inspiring aircraft.

Thankfully, the swan continues to grace our skies – a crisper white than the cirrus clouds under which it flies – though not all year round. For six weeks of the year it takes on the flightless status of its grounded sister aircraft.

Exhausted from the effort of finding a mate, finding a nesting site, fending off competitors, fending off predators and caring for fluffy cygnets, the swan finally takes a break in July or August as the moulting season begins. The cob and pen take it in turns to moult, ensuring one can fly while the other defends the brood. Usually, it's a case of 'ladies first' while the cob stays put to guard the cygnets. Incredibly, all it takes is four missing outer feathers from the wing or tail to ground a swan,[5] highlighting again what a finely tuned flying machine it is. We already know it is a few grams away from being too heavy to fly, but it can also be rendered flightless merely by losing a few vital feathers. The moulting process sees the fresh healthy feathers push out the old scruffy quills, worn down from water, sun, constant preening and numerous battles. It's a gradual process to ensure there are no bald patches which would otherwise make it unable to swim as well as fly.

Swans lose five per cent of their bodyweight when moulting and are left vulnerable to enemies. Unable to flee to the sky, the bird must stand and fight any predators who head their way. Just as the female eats copiously before starting to incubate the eggs, so the pair gorge themselves on weeds in the days before moulting.

As for non-breeding swans, the one- and two-year-olds often flock together to moult in the safety of numbers. This often takes place earlier than in breeding pairs. In Denmark, huge numbers of native mute swans – sometimes tens of thousands – gather in the coastal areas to moult en masse.

For the vast majority of mutes in the UK, the moulting process is merely a chance to ready themselves for the season ahead in a country they call home 365 days a year. But for some in northern Europe and the icy plains of Siberia, they must ready themselves for a long journey.

Mute swans are not known for migrating the huge distances, or in the large numbers, flown by their whooper and Bewick's cousins. And maybe that's a sensible choice, as migration comes with risks. In April 2020, thousands of swallows and swifts were left dead after attempting to migrate from Africa to Europe for the springtime breeding season. Strong, cold winds and rain battered the birds as they passed over the Aegean Sea. Many simply vanished while hundreds were found dead from exhaustion on the streets and balconies of Athens. Others managed to limp to smaller Greek islands where they were rescued by concerned locals and conservation groups.

British swans are mostly safe from such large-scale disasters despite extensive travel within our borders. Swans have been known to head for coastal areas during harsh winters where the salty waters are less likely to freeze. But the longest distances are flown by mute swans escaping the icy darkness of Siberia, heading to the warmer lands of southern Europe. Where they do, they fly in huge V-formations, sometimes reaching heights of 10,000 feet. They fly for days on end, stopping only briefly to rest and to feed. They cover double the distance managed by Concorde on its former route from London to New York, and they do it with less fuel and less noise. What a bird!

Up and down

17 May 2016
Cities with populations of more than 10 million people, or a population density of 2,000 per square kilometre, are known as megacities. There are only 33 in the world.

London is one of the greenest. The UK's capital contains 35,000 acres of public parks, woodlands and gardens, making it one of the greenest major cities on the planet.

London boasts more than just parks; it also features strategically built bird habitats. The London Wetland Centre on the south bank of the River Thames at Barnes, is one of the best examples. This 100-acre site uses four abandoned Victorian reservoirs to give nature a home. The centre combines a mixture of woodlands, marshland, reedbeds, scrub and lakes to attract a huge array of wildlife. Many of its birds cannot be found anywhere else in London. Commonly spotted species include bittern, pintail duck, lapwing, water rail, ring-necked parakeet, sparrowhawk, sand martin, kingfisher, little grebe and great crested grebe. Incredibly this site, run by the Wildfowl and Wetlands Trust, is just a 15-minute train journey from central London, so I bunk off early from work one Friday afternoon and head straight there.

The afternoon is calm and still, the reeds swaying gently from the weak westerly breeze. Only the honking of greylag geese and the unmistakable explosive call of a Cetti's warbler can be heard. This tiny brown bird has eluded me for decades, always heard but never seen. I heard it first at the age of ten. It was a rare find for Berkshire. Twitchers from far and wide descended on Thatcham's Kennet and Avon Canal to hear the powerful 'pwit, pity-chewit, chewit, chewit' or to catch a glimpse as it skulked among a labyrinth of reeds and branches.

Now, 30 years on, it is thankfully a familiar resident to our marshlands, reedbeds and scrublands. In that time I have heard around 50, but have seen not one. Once again it bellows out its song. Such a bullish noise from such a tiny creature – the noisy Jack Russell of the bird world. I make myself dizzy scanning the tall reeds for movement, the tall thin brown lines swinging like barcodes through my binoculars until my vision becomes blurred. At last, it darts atop a quill to explode with song once more – a short-lived appearance – before scurrying back among the wall of reeds and bullrushes. It is my first sight of this noisy little bird in three decades of trying. Could things get any better?

Three hundred feet above, a far more dramatic scene is unfolding. A peregrine falcon is flying from right to left, surveying the scene below. Its flight is frenetic – short, sharp wingbeats propel it through the sky at impressive speed with only a very occasional glide. While other raptors gently soar before switching into hunting mode, the peregrine has a twitchy, agitated demeanour, forever a threat to anything in its sights, its wings jerking and flexing. Two hundred feet below this sinister silhouette, ten sand martins and five swallows dance like fireflies in the sky, gorging on the aphids and midges drifting up from the water in the warm rising air.

At first, I struggle to work out whether the falcon is hunting or commuting. Soon all becomes clear. With a slash of its wings it climbs for a split second before plummeting into a stoop. I have read that peregrines like to attack with the sun behind them, blinding their prey from the imminent attack. If this is the plan, it has failed.

The swallows and martins dive as one towards the safety of the water. Peregrines are easily spooked by people, and there are far too many visitors around for the falcon to continue the pursuit. Besides, catching a swallow or a martin is hard work compared to its staple diet of more slovenly prey such as starlings and pigeons. Instead it retreats across the Thames to the rooftop of Charing Cross Hospital, where it is known to nest.

At the Wetland Centre, the falcon's dive has sent pied wagtails, mallards and pigeons into the sky. Wigeon ducks are screaming 'wee-ooo', the redshanks wailing their 'tew-tew' alarm. But why? The danger has passed.

A pair of collared doves bathing in the morning sun rise in terror from the water's edge. Their flight is laboured yet urgent, the gentle whistling sound of their wings unable to disguise their panic. The pair split – the first toward me, the second flying low and true like an arrow toward the lake's small island. I fix my eyes on the first one as it weaves – left then right, up then down – toward the bridge on which I'm standing. It's over in less than ten seconds as the silhouette of a female sparrowhawk skilfully cuts off the dove's escape, crashing into the bird at speed with a dull, sickening crack. She uses all her might to rise to safety, but the dove is too heavy. No amount of flapping can prevent her from sinking, which she does until finally thumping down with her prey less than 15 metres from my position. Aware of my presence, she immediately covers the struggling dove with her wings and pecks and pulls at the nape of the dove's neck until the struggle is over.

But this is not to be a relaxing meal. Exposed and threatened on the footpath, the female gorges on her catch, ripping huge fleshy chunks from the neck and flank, scanning the horizon for magpies or crows that could so easily steal her prize.

I watch the grizzly scene unfold for five minutes as the feathers of the once-beautiful dove tumble across the path into the reeds, which just moments ago had framed my first Cetti's warbler. So many birdwatching trips end in disappointment. So many hours spent in awful weather, trudging through mud and tall grass, freezing in hides, fingers numb from the cold wind. Not today. I am almost overwhelmed by the relentless drama, but the best is yet to come.

The avid hawk is aware long before I am. In one tidy motion, she drags and hides the carcass in the long grass and takes to the air, vanishing through a small gap between a fence and a reedbed. As I return my gaze to the water, framed by reeds on either side, a cob and pen begin their take-off run, oblivious to the meal they have disturbed. Once again, their regal demeanour makes me grin a wry smile. They are too important to notice the less impressive birds of this world fighting for scraps. They have places to go and things to see.

Swans usually need around five metres to take off on water (plus another 15 if they want to avoid obstacles such as houses). This pair appear to have plenty to spare as they head towards me, stamping their feet through the water, furiously beating their wings. Their bodies are perfectly horizontal, necks in front, fully extended. They have been running for 10 metres and look nowhere near ready. Swans give the impression of lacking acceleration. How can that bulky white frame possibly become airborne? But airborne they are, as 15 metres from where I stand they finally leave the water, swinging to my left, their right wingtips skating the water as their bellies are exposed. They have timed their launch to perfection, steering clear of my position and skimming the bird hide as they rise gently into the dusky skies.

Chapter Six

THE INSPIRATION

Armed with a cheese roll supply fit for a small army and a gallon of tomato soup, I plonk myself in an Essex hide with the sun behind me to find the mute swans waddling along the muddy banks of a small marsh. It is New Year's Day 2018.

The swans look like they are roughly two or three years in age, meaning I am probably looking at a new couple. I decide to imagine they are fresh lovers, a budding young pair preparing to raise their first young.

During the three hours that pass, I watch them forage for weeds, providing for one another. I note the extraordinary flexibility of their necks, the way they flip them back at awkward angles to pluck out the weed in hard-to-reach places. I notice how this pair seem less eager than most swans to duck their heads underwater, instead dragging their feet through the mud before dipping down to pluck their winnings from the surface.

I listen to them express their affection through gargles and snorts, and watch how in the blink of an eye they can flick from love and compassion to naked aggression when a Canada goose strolls too close.

As the sun begins to drop behind my tall wooden hide, the pair's demeanour softens and their activity slows. Propped in the shallows of the dirty marsh, the cob and pen approach one another, shuffling more than swimming. Less than a metre apart they gently slow to a halt and lightly arch back their necks before smoothly bowing their heads. With an air of tender sensitivity, they edge closer and closer still. In unison they sway their heads from side to side, up and down, back and forth... then rest bill-to-bill before arching back their necks once more to form the perfect heart in the glow of the pink evening sun.

I watch the scene unfold with complete and utter concentration. Not once does my heartrate spike. Not once do I lose focus. Not once does my hand reach for the camera. I am living in the present. Not the past, not the future. When I do this, the power of swans is untold.

———

I cannot stress enough the importance of 'enjoying the moment' when observing nature, focusing on what you actually see rather than what you want to see. It's something that has only recently become clear in my mind. I have lost count of the number of beautiful moments ruined by my stressed and desperate attempts to capture the perfect photograph. I wince at the hours I have lost staring at the camera's settings or preview screens when I could have been enjoying the beauty, grace and behaviour of the wildlife laid out before me. I grimace at the moments I have missed while buried in a phone, sending bird photos to friends – tasks that could have waited until the evening. My number one piece of advice to any budding birdwatcher could not be simpler

– keep your head up and your mind present. Regrets and resentments are dangerous emotions, best avoided, but there is one incident I simply cannot shake off. It occurred exactly a year before that moment with the heart-shaped swans, and in the very same hide.

New Year's Day 2017 was my fourth trip to the RSPB's Rainham Marshes Nature Reserve in as many weeks. My search for barn and short-eared owls had proved fruitless until the afternoon sun began to fade on this cold, bitter day. My fingers were freezing, my cheese rolls were all eaten, my soup flask empty and my spirits low. As I trudged along the boardwalks in the direction of the car park, something caught my eye above the rugged grassland to my left. Quartering across the meadows, this stunning bird was on the hunt for mice among the dishevelled grass. A mottled yellow-brown on top, paler underneath and with long rounded wings. From a distance of 100 yards I could still make out the wide yellow eyes and the shrew nestled tightly in its talons. At last, a short-eared owl.

As I reached for my camera, a second bird swooped in from the side mobbing the owl and sending it spiralling towards the ground. Pale in comparison, but similar in size, what could it be? A herring gull perhaps? A raptor of some kind?

In fact I was watching a barn owl and a short-eared owl squabbling in mid-air over the same prey. At the exact same moment I also realised my camera settings were fixed for the sunny light of the previous hour, not the murky light which had since descended. As I scrambled for the correct settings, the lens cap fell into the mud. As I knelt down to retrieve it, my glasses suffered a similar fate.

I continued to fiddle aimlessly with buttons and touch screens, my anxiety rising with every passing second. Following each failed photo, I checked my screen, adjusted the shutter speed, raised the ISO, shot another terrible photo and continued the pattern again and again. By the time I had achieved a photograph in which it was clear a bird was flying, let alone that it featured two owls, the moment had passed. The two owls disappeared behind a hide across the site, a performance now to be enjoyed by birders less foolish than me.

If I could turn back the clock, I would simply reach for my binoculars. I could observe the slow, creepy flight of the barn owl – appearing forever to be on the point of stalling and dropping from the sky. As for the short-eared owl, I could enjoy the stiff beats of its round wings, often compared to moths and butterflies. Above all, I could watch the unfolding battle between these two magnificent hunters until one of them escaped with the spoils. Instead, not only did I return home without a decent photo, but also without a memory to be cherished.

It's possible, in fact probable, that I will never again see a short-eared owl battling a barn owl in the skies above Britain. Although a minor event in the grand scheme of life, it was a watershed moment, as I could suddenly see what happens when a hobby that is supposed to be a source of contentment, even joy, is allowed to become an obsessive source of stress and anxiety.

Of course, the birds were not to blame, nor their propensity for staying out of view. I was the problem. I was spending huge swathes of my life doing things I didn't want to do or being in places I didn't want to be. Yet here I was, lucky enough to do exactly what I wanted, lucky enough to have the money to visit Rainham Marshes four times in four weeks and to have the health to walk around this incredible place surrounded by incredible birds. But I was still miserable.

It's true that in the first three attempts I had not seen a single owl – my main goal – yet I had seen and heard scores of curlews with their incredible bubbling calls. I'd watched a flock of more than 200 wigeon ducks whirring around the hides with their fascinating 'whe-o' screams. And I had noted two young greylag geese rubbing heads, entwining their long necks and simply enjoying one another's presence. Had I enjoyed these moments or displayed any gratitude? Not one iota. I had become fixated with what I wanted to see rather than what I was actually seeing.

I had been telling my friends, family and anyone else who would listen that my wholesome hobby was a beautifully calming influence – a mental health saviour and the perfect antidote for a stressful job in the heart of the city. But the truth was that I was carrying my fears, resentments and compulsive behaviours into the bird hides and marshes of Essex. I was rarely enjoying my trips to the marshlands of Kent or the heathlands of the New Forest. Instead the anxious thoughts from work were intoxicating my birdwatching. The deadlines, the quest for perfection and the search for approval from peers which dominated my office life were translating into quests for the rarest bird or the perfect photo, and then an obsessive urge to share my successes immediately with the world.

The incident with the owls was, of course, not serious in itself. There had been far more extreme warning signs in my behaviour in the preceding months, but to detail those would make this a very different book. But it was this moment which spurred me to get help and work to live in the present. This battle began in earnest the very next day. Exactly one year later and I was watching those two amazing swans for three hours, learning of the great joy to be had when you cherish what is right in front of you.

Walking outdoors, swan watching and birdwatching as sources of physical and mental health are hardly groundbreaking concepts. To paraphrase Socrates in Plato's *Republic:*

> *In order for man to succeed in life, God provided him with two means, education*

and physical activity. Not separately, one
for the soul and the other for the body,
but for the two together. With these
means, man can attain perfection. 🙶

Yet too often we become swept up in the chaos of life and forget to truly care for ourselves. A daily walk outside is an absolute necessity for me – as important as drinking water or breathing air. I am lucky the desire to throw a pair of binoculars around my neck and a pair of boots on my feet and to open the front door is greater than the darker forces in my mind. More often than not I can regather perspective and manage my thoughts – not everyone can.

Nature will never 'cure' me or allow me to 'win', but walking outdoors helps me decipher the difference between the reality on the ground and the terrors invented by my mind. Nature offers the space I need to gently consider problems rather than obsessing and panicking about them.

I can become overwhelmed with loneliness when sitting in an empty room, grasping at negative thoughts and amplifying them in an anxious frenzy. Yet when sitting in an empty bird hide, I find myself alone but not lonely; mindful of what's actually in front of me – the swans – not what I imagine may be in front of me – disaster and pain. Birdwatching reminds me I am not the centre of the universe, merely a tiny part of something far greater.

I compare my healthy head to Thatcham Lakes, where the swans represent my troubles. They fly in for a brief visit, land, are acknowledged, and then fly away. The more I visit Thatcham Lakes, the more I know where those dangerous tree roots and potholes lie, even if from time to time they are obscured by the snow.

As the years have passed, my birdwatching has become a good barometer for my health. When I get frustrated at my less-than-perfect photographs, I know it's time to put down the camera. When I have spent an hour searching and scanning the reeds for a bittern, but have missed two kingfishers and myriad waders and warblers, I know it's time to release the scope and enjoy the landscape with the naked eye.

When I am getting as much enjoyment from a robin as a peregrine, I know all is well. When I take the time to watch the warmth and love between two mute swans, I am living in the present.

I tell this story not to tout birdwatching as a cure for all mental struggles, nor to besmirch the hobby of amateur wildlife photography, but to caveat the following technical advice with the far more important birdwatching plea to enjoy the moment. It's a lot more fun and a lot more rewarding!

Having said that, once you have observed the birds, enjoyed their quirks, felt your heartrate lower and the sun and wind on your face, feel free to use the following tips to grab a decent swan photo:

1. Underexpose

White birds can be difficult to photograph. The most common mistake sees photographers lower the shutter speed to secure the crisp whiteness of its feathers. On closer inspection you will find there is almost no detail in the image. This means you are essentially left with a photo of a beautifully fresh white blob. Remember it is much easier to edit an underexposed photo than it is an overexposed one.

To put this into perspective, I once came perilously close to deleting a photograph of a swan because it looked too dark and underexposed on the preview screen. I decided to retain the image in the slim hope it could be rescued with a bit of editing when I got home. It is now the bestselling and most viewed photograph on my website www.ilikebird.uk (see picture 1)

Try to avoid taking photos of swans during the blazing midday sun. There is a high risk the swan will simply become too reflective, making it impossible to capture the detail of the feathers. Bright sunshine also creates harsh distracting shadows while small clouds can play havoc with your settings as the light switches from bright to dark to bright. Instead, it's often easier to take photos on a bright overcast day when the light is consistent and the shadows nice and soft.

2. Focus on the eye

This applies to all wildlife photography. If the eye of the animal is in your shot, make sure this is the bit which is perfectly in focus. It helps bring the image to life. This does not necessarily mean the eye needs to be in the centre of the shot. If your camera focusses on the spot in the middle of the view finder, simply ensure the eye is in focus and then move the camera to place the eye where you want it. If the swan is reasonably still, then take the shot.

3. Get level

In most cases your photos will look best when you are level with the swan. More often than not you will find yourself looking down at swans – either from a river bank, a bird hide or a bridge. If it is possible to safely descend to their level you will find the shot has more character, more impact and more detail. In some cases, getting below the swan can convey the sheer size of the bird. Wide-angle lenses are also great at capturing the swan's surroundings.

4. Do your research

It's always worth checking where people have taken good pictures of swans in your local area. While there are plenty of swans to go around, many are in places that are not easily accessible or where you can't get close enough to take a good photograph. Local social media accounts and groups offer a fantastic way to stay updated on the progress of nests and broods. While Instagram is fantastic for photographs, you'll probably find more information and updates on Twitter or Facebook. Cobs are at their most active and interesting once the eggs have been laid or hatched. They are busy scouring for food for the pen and are highly protective of the nest. This presents a whole host of photographic opportunities – chasing geese across the lake and hissing at humans, as well as more tender shots, such as feeding the pen.

Remember to check the weather forecast and don't be put off by clouds, storms or the cold. As long as you're well prepared to protect your camera, your health and your safety, the weather can add real emotion and character to your photographs.

Finally, make a careful note of the sunrise and sunset times. Both these periods offer an atmospheric light – photographers call it the golden hour – which can enhance all kinds of wildlife photography. It's also fair to state that birds are generally at their most active at dawn and dusk. Predators do most of their hunting during these hours, opting to rest during the warmer daytime period.

5. Increase the aperture

Some of the best wildlife photos create the effect of the subject popping out of the image against a soft, blurred background. This is known as the bokeh effect. The technique is particularly useful when the subject – in this case a swan – is swimming in a busy area – maybe surrounded by ducks, reeds or tree branches. It ensures the swan is in focus while the less important clutter nearby is blurred. This gives the impression the subject is pin sharp.

To achieve this you need to select a wide-aperture setting on your camera, which basically means selecting the lowest 'f' number available on your camera settings. Experiment using low and high 'f' numbers on your camera. You will soon realise that having a narrow aperture (a high 'f' number) allows the sticks, reeds and ducks to distract from the main event – the swan.

To improve this effect still further, you should always try to position yourself so that the distance between the swan and the clutter is as long as possible. Sometimes it helps to place a feeding station in a strategic location. But always bear in mind the first ethic of wildlife photography: you must not disturb the natural world.

Finally, it will come as no surprise to read that being close to your subject helps. Even the more powerful telephoto lenses will capture better images the closer you are to the swan. If you can creep a few feet closer to a cob without being noticed or putting him, yourself or others in danger, the rewards can be enormous.

Bonus tip: Try not to go overboard with this technique. There will be many occasions when the swan's surroundings are just as impressive as the swan itself, so why blur them out? If you find yourself staring at a swan beside a glorious pink cherry blossom tree with the spring sunshine setting in the distance, you may have stumbled across the perfect landscape scene for your living room wall. Using the bokeh effect is a fantastic technique. But remember to take a few without it as well (see picture 16).

6. Be patient

Swans are easier to photograph than most birds for the simple reason that they are tamer and more tolerant of the presence of humans. They are also easier to spot, move more slowly than small birds and are found among some of the country's most picturesque surroundings.

Despite all of this, there are certain coveted shots. Wildlife photographers around the world have for many decades attempted to master the art of photographing swans:

a) Flying
b) Rising from the water while spreading their wings
c) Leading their cygnets across the water in a perfect line
d) Meeting one another head-on to form a heart shape.

All four require a huge amount of patience, a dollop of camera trickery and a slice of luck.

I once sat on the bank of a pond in Richmond for five days before finally managing to capture an angry cob rising from the water, wings outstretched, in a clear display of power. It took the first three days just to begin to understand its habits and behaviours.

I noticed it had a favoured area of the pond, which presumably had a healthy supply of weeds. He seemed to be most active between 3 p.m. and 5 p.m. when greylag and Egyptian geese were at their boldest, daring to land in the pond and take advantage of the bread thrown by tourists. I learned there was a sweet spot between 4 p.m. and 4.30 p.m. when the sun was behind me, lighting up this particular part of the water. My viewpoint worked well as the background consisted of trees and bushes rather than buildings or human joggers in their neon activewear.

As the hours and days passed I continually updated the shutter speed and ISO in line with the weather and light, testing my settings on the cob, waiting for it to perform. Finally, on day five, two Egyptian geese announced themselves with deafening honks, passing over some nearby houses and down toward the pond. They had barely touched down before the cob attacked, heaving his huge body toward them with powerful strokes of his enormous feet. He recoiled his long slinky neck like a cobra before lunging at the first goose with his hard bill, ripping out its tail feathers with frightening force. The pair had seen enough and immediately skedaddled, fleeing toward a neighbouring meadow. The cob took its pursuit from the water to the air, chasing them at low level into the scruffy grass. Only when the geese were more than 100 yards away did the swan land among the dry tufts and molehills before beginning his ungainly waddle back to the water. This was my moment.

I had noticed in the seconds after a successful chase, this cob tended to make a series of gargling and snorting noises before ducking his head and body underwater. He would often proceed to shake off the droplets before pushing himself vertically out of the water and flapping his wings.

Now he made his way back into the pond, snorting with vigour, before making a beeline for the exact spot in which he seemed to enjoy feeding at around 4 p.m. Right on cue, he dipped his head, turned to face me, the afternoon sun reflecting off his moist, glistening body, rising powerfully from the water, his bill now turned upward to the wispy cirrus clouds above us.

With a loud chortled grunt he spread his wings, flapping them gently at first, but with increasing speed until an audible ferocity drowned out the grunts with the 'wou-wou' of beating feathers and the 'slap-slap' of wings on water. (see picture 10) Five flaps later and his display of power was over as he settled back to the surface and continued to feed. A family of five people arrived at the water's edge just a minute later, oblivious to the drama which had taken place and even passing comment on how tranquil everything was.

But I was confident I had grabbed my shot, having switched the camera to 'continuous shooting' mode. This meant that once the swan was in focus, I merely had to keep my finger firmly pressed on the shutter button rather than repeatedly hitting it. The flapping of clamorous wings had lasted only five seconds. In this time I had taken more than 20 photographs.

7. Photograph swans in flight

We have discussed the importance of using the correct light and surroundings, but the wind is also a vital consideration.

You may have noticed that when flocks of birds are perched on the ground, a fence or a telephone wire, they tend to face the same direction. If you are particularly observant you may also have twigged that more often than not, they are facing into the wind.

Scientists suggest this ensures their feathers do not become ruffled. Most of the quills are positioned to ensure minimum air resistance when travelling forward. If birds were to turn their backs on the wind, they would quickly become engulfed by a bundle of fluff and feathers.

Another reason to face the wind relates to flight. Similar to aircraft, swans take off and land into the wind. This ensures that a sufficient amount of air passes over their wings to allow them to generate the lift needed for take-off. When landing, it ensures they can slow to a speed which allows them to hit their touchdown target rather than skidding off into a hedge, a wall or, worse still, a road.

This information is vital for swan photographers. If you know your local swans land on a lake at dawn and depart at dusk, you can use the wind to determine in which direction they are likely to travel. If the sun is shining from the same direction as from where the wind is blowing, you have hit the jackpot. If it's the exact opposite and you're facing the sun, you may consider altering your position to create a diagonal view as the swan takes off. Alternatively, you may choose to get down low and use the swan to block out the sun to create an arty, backlit effect, the sun lighting up the feathers from behind.

Next you need to consider your camera settings. While swans fly at slower speeds than many birds, their wings are beating fast and their feet are pedalling furiously on take-off. In short, there are a lot of moving parts that could become blurred. To avoid this, you must select the highest-possible shutter speed without underexposing (darkening) the shot too much. Again, continuous shooting is a good option here. But if you do decide to shoot in single-shot mode when side-on to the swan, try to take the shot when the wing is at its highest or lowest so that you can see the head.

Finally, composition is crucial. One of the biggest mistakes I made during my early days as a photographer was putting a moving animal in the centre of the frame. On nearly every occasion I ended up with a perfectly focused shot of a headless bird. Instead aim to hit the shutter button with room to spare. In other words, when lining up the shot in your screen, give the swan space into which it can fly. Not only does this prevent shots of headless birds, it also avoids photos that look crowded.

8. Use the reflections

Always take note of the water's surface. The fewer ripples, the more chance you have of capturing the perfect mirror image. Remember to take a mixture of portrait and landscape shots. There is nothing worse than returning home to realise there was a perfect swan reflection which you chopped in half because you were shooting landscape.

9. Use tripods and monopods

If like me you have a shaky hand, then a stabiliser of some kind is essential. Tripods allow you to take photos with almost zero camera shake, giving you the best chance of a pin-sharp image. However, carting one around all morning can be tiring work and risks turning a relaxing, enjoyable day into a physical ordeal. Instead, I prefer to carry my camera on a lighter monopod which, unlike a tripod, doesn't need adjusting every time I spot a bird. It is also lighter, rests nicely on my shoulder when walking and still offers a decent amount of stability when taking photos. Possibly its biggest advantage is in being more manoeuvrable than a tripod, which is hugely helpful when those pesky swans won't stay still.

10. Use the rule of thirds

Most cameras allow you to divide your view into a grid of nine equally sized rectangles. The four corners of the central box are often good spots to place the main subject of your photograph – maybe the eye of the swan or the weed in its bill. Once again, try to avoid the photo looking claustrophobic. If the swan is facing to your left, consider placing its head on one of the two corners on the right-hand side of the central box. This allows plenty of space into which the swan can stare. Placing it on the left will give a tight, cluttered feel to the image.

So there it is. Go forth and snap away to your heart's content – but the key word really is *content*. My advice would be to stay present with nature and limit your fascination with techniques, buttons and settings. The minute you begin to feel tense or stressed, you should watch the bird with your naked eyes. The moment you are missing that passing kingfisher, that hunting owl or those adoring swans – well, the time has come to put... down... the... camera.

Chapter Seven

THE FUTURE

Around 74,000 mute swans are currently swimming, flying and waddling around the British Isles. According to the RSPB, roughly 12,800 of them are thought to be breeding. Although swan numbers are in better shape than many British birds, the charity has placed the species on its 'amber' list, meaning it is in moderate decline. Humans are almost exclusively to blame.

We have ruthlessly betrayed swans, taking advantage of their trusting nature and acting as multi-pronged instruments of destruction. Over the centuries, we have polluted their waterways, vandalised their nests, introduced predators such as cats and dogs and at one point even hunted them to the brink of extinction. But our most damaging crime has been to build on their homes.

Swans need wasteland and wetlands to thrive. In recent decades, huge swathes of land have been built upon. In other cases, the homes of swans have been left untouched but nearby manmade complexes have ruined the delicately balanced water-table and drainage systems, destroying habitat. Where this is the case, cobs and pens will struggle to raise a healthy brood or, worse still, won't even bother trying. They may even fly further afield in search of suitable nesting sites in unfamiliar places. Such journeys put them at risk of succumbing to other dangers such as roads, pylons and buildings. Sadly, for those swans lucky or skilful enough to avoid this minefield of physical hazards, there are yet more perils – some of them invisible.

While I was writing this book the world was embroiled in a global pandemic. At times during that period, almost a third of the global population was in lockdown, with people unable to leave their homes except for emergencies, essential errands and short bursts of exercise. The World Health Organisation had instructed people to observe 'social distancing', borders were closed, businesses shut down and hospitals stretched like never before.

On this occasion the culprit was a coronavirus. Next time it could be bird flu. This is one existential threat from which we can do very little to protect swans. Avian influenza, more commonly known as bird flu, is highly infectious among many birds. While it seems that turkeys, chickens, geese and swans are most susceptible, any bird can catch it. Symptoms include lack of appetite, breathing problems, swelling of the head, discharge from the eyes, diarrhoea and depression. The death rate is high, but some recover naturally and many domesticated birds are treated and survive. In 2018, seven of the Queen's Windsor swans are thought to have died from bird flu.

The nightmare scenario, however, is not a mass outbreak among birds, but a mutation which renders it transmissible to humans. Most scientists agree this is exactly what happened in 1918. A lethal bird-flu strain infected 500 million people, a quarter of the world's population at that time, and killed up to 50 million. The virus was better known as the Spanish flu.*

Similar to birds hitting aircraft, it is not the flu itself which poses the biggest threat to swans – after all, many recover – but the human reaction to it. The Spanish flu ravaged the world for three years but was not well understood. Nowadays, when smaller outbreaks occur, large numbers of domestic birds are culled to stop the spread, and migrating birds are also killed.

The most potent recent example occurred in Russia in October 2018 when 80 outbreaks were reported. Millions of mostly domestic birds were culled, along with flocks of birds known to migrate long distances, such as swans and geese. While it's true that UK populations tend to stay put, there are tens of thousands of mute swans moving huge distances around Europe, Asia and, in some cases, north Africa. If bird flu were to spread around the globe, swans would struggle to escape its direct and indirect effects.

Another invisible threat is of course climate change. Surprisingly, there is so far little evidence of swans being affected by global heating, but urban heat has most

---

* The name 'Spanish flu' is misleading. The main countries fighting the First World War are thought to have censored the press and drastically downplayed the devastating effects of the pandemic at home to preserve morale. Instead, they gave the media the green light to report on neutral Spain – in particular the plight of its gravely ill King Alfonso XIII (he survived the illness). This is how it became known as the Spanish flu.

certainly had an impact. Many birds resident in London – not just swans – appear to be breeding earlier in the year. The many thousands of buildings trap and retain warmth, while the cars, trucks, trains and factories all produce heat too. While birds in the countryside are hunkering down in the late winter days, London birds have a spring in their step and a head start in the breeding process. For those species which might consider a second brood – like the swan – city heat means the autumn chill comes later too, thus widening the breeding window.

Bacterial diseases are another big threat to swans. Avian botulism is a toxin produced in a 'perfect storm' of warm, oxygen-deprived water and decaying animals. It spreads to weeds and fish before being passed up the food chain. While the problem is much more severe in hot areas of North America and Japan, outbreaks have occurred in the UK. Most ducks, geese and swans will die relatively quickly from this distressing illness.

Various parasites and leeches can also pose problems, but nothing that the mute swan as a species cannot handle. After all, the swan is a survivor. Wildlife author Adam Nicolson once said that 'in the long dance of extinction and continuity, there are some birds that stand as symbols of persistence'. The swan surely stands as one of the biggest and most dazzling of those symbols. Confronting brutal challenges over many thousands of years, this magical bird has found ways to adapt and evolve. The Ice

Age saw it learn to fly huge distances to escape the deadly grip of winters far more bitter than anything we are used to. In our own time, it has learned to use human litter to build nests.

It is hard to think of many other British animals with which British people share such a complex relationship. With swans we have simultaneously protected and plundered, glorified and hunted, revered and destroyed. We have nurtured and sold them, watched them in awe, but turned them into meals, toys and hats.

At times the swan's evolution has been aided by its beauty and its air of majesty in the eyes of humans. One can't help but wonder what its fate would have been had King Edward IV not decided to claim so many of these magnificent birds for himself with the stroke of a pen. Was it this selfish act which saved the swan from the fate suffered by the stork, the osprey and the red kite, which at one time or another all became extinct in England? Would Edward have done this if swans were not so pleasing to the eye?

Swans are truly entangled in our way of life. They have shown a great ability to adapt in the face of more people, homes and cars gobbling up the land. But as the saying goes, they aren't making any more of it, and nowadays there is simply not enough habitat to go around. Swans, like many other creatures, are struggling to survive in a country full of manmade death traps. However, there is hope.

We Britons are more caring toward animals than most developed societies. We were the first in the world to set up a welfare charity for animals when in 1824 the Society for the Prevention of Cruelty to Animals was established. In 1840, Queen Victoria bestowed royal status on the charity, and the RSPCA is still going strong today.* The Royal Society for the Protection of Birds (RSPB) was established half a century later, in 1889, and today our legislation protecting wildlife is stronger than in most countries. The same is true of our animal-testing laws.

We are also a nation of gardeners, of animal observers and of bird feeders. There are huge numbers of non-birdwatchers who care passionately about our feathered friends. The British Trust for Ornithology estimates half of all UK households regularly feed the birds that visit their gardens. In fact, we are thought to buy between 50,000 and 60,000 tonnes of bird food every year – that's two kilograms per home. While garden food is of little help to swans, this does show a desire to nurture our birdlife that is widely shared.

Meanwhile, RSPB subscriptions and donations are on the up. The work of conservation charities is invaluable, as are the people who support them. Most of us do not

* It is worth noting that the National Society for the Prevention of Cruelty to Children (NSPCC) was not founded until 60 years later. That's how much we love our animals!

possess the energy, skill or time to clear out huge swathes of land for swans. But we can all support the charities and organisations that do. They have the resources, expertise and manpower to buy land, repurpose it, maintain it and, crucially, fight developers in court to preserve it. Whether it is volunteering or donating, they need our help. RSPB Rainham Marshes Nature Reserve is a great example of how disused land can be transformed into habitat for a wide range of species. In the year 2000, the charity bought 411 hectares of land from the Ministry of Defence, which no longer needed them as a firing range. The Essex site in the Thames Estuary now features wet grassland, ditches, lakes and a huge array of plant life perfect for swans and a plethora of bird and wildlife. It is now one of the most popular birdwatching sites in the country, visited by thousands of people every year, and features a wide range of educational activities for children. It is always encouraging to see people birdwatching, but particularly so when children are taking an interest. The more we understand about the natural world, the more invested we become in preserving it.

Which brings us to another force for good – education.

A recent survey by Natural England found that fewer than a quarter of children regularly use their local 'patch of nature', compared to over half of all adults when they were children. It also showed that fewer than one in ten children regularly play in wild places.

A separate report by the National Trust suggested children spend so little time outdoors that only half can tell the difference between a bee and a wasp and that one in three cannot identify a magpie. The same study showed nine out of ten children can recognise a Dalek. In fact, according to the Wild Network, in 2016 three-quarters of UK children were spending less time outdoors than prison inmates.

Not everyone has a nature reserve on their doorstep, nor can everyone afford a pair of walking boots or binoculars. Some people may not have the time or health to travel to the woods or a forest. So the secret is to integrate nature into our lives and the lives of our children – even in the smallest of ways. I lived in central London for five years, but still spotted frogs and toads in the parks at night as well as foxes in the morning. In Peckham in south-east London I heard wrens during the day and tawny owls at dusk. A longer walk to Lewisham and I could see herons fishing in the Ravensbourne River and stunning kingfishers at dawn. One spring, I even put up a bird box on the windowsill of my flat and watched a pair of blue tits raise five chicks. Five chicks in one of the biggest metropolises on the planet!

Nature is everywhere, so we can easily nurture and cherish it wherever we happen to be – whether it's a spider's web in our doorway or a pigeon on the roof. I try not to let the weather distract me. It's easy to appreciate nature in the spring sunshine when the grass and trees are awash with green, but birds and other creatures are just as easy to spot in the winter when the leaves and foliage that hide them in the summertime have fallen to the ground. Remember the late Duke of Edinburgh's motto: 'There is no such thing as bad weather – only inappropriate clothing.' Many birdwatchers, including myself, would possibly disagree. Wind is horrible, and most birds hate it too. But hurricanes aside, we can always get outside and immerse ourselves in whatever nature provides. We don't need to become ornithologists overnight and we won't enjoy it all, but we can treasure what works for us and leave the rest for others to love.

If you have learned anything from this book, then feel free to share your knowledge with whoever will listen, including your children. One of the most rewarding ways I now spend my time is hosting walk-and-talks along English rivers. Once again, I feel compelled to point out that I am not an ornithologist. But sharing the knowledge I do possess is hugely satisfying; I only hope the people in my walk-and-talk groups pass it on. The more we know about swans, and the more people who know it, the better the chances of protecting them, because it's hard to care for and protect what we don't understand. If just one person leaves one of my walks knowing the difference between a male and a female mute swan, or can tell a blue tit call from that of a great tit, then I'm happy. Aside from that, it's always great fun when someone sends you a bird picture and asks you what it is.

Thankfully, today conservation is taken slightly more seriously by politicians than in years gone by, but it's still not enough. They will only act when the people who elect them put pressure on them to act. In short, our environment will only become a priority in politics when we make it one. By immersing ourselves in nature and educating ourselves about it, we can help preserve the swan – an emblem and spirit of our waterways and skies.

EPILOGUE

You may recall from this book's prologue my account of five swans landing on a partially frozen lake in spectacular fashion in my Berkshire hometown of Thatcham. The scene did not end there.

After watching them touch down on the ice, sending ducks scattering into the sky, I slowly made my way around the lake toward them. The creak of packed ice beneath my feet turned to a muffled thud as the powder snow filled every crevice in the grip of the soles of my boots. I stopped to kick my boots against a small willow tree, freeing the dirty ice from my shoes, then regained my balance to continue my journey.

Our ability to walk long distances on two legs is perhaps what first separated us from the rest of the apes, freeing up our hands to use tools. At the dawn of humanity, it was hammerstones and sharp stone knives; now it's binoculars.

Walking is an asset I try never to take for granted. So often it has kept me physically and mentally fit. Walking brings a serenity which so often seems out of reach. Traditional meditation is not for me, but walking brings a calmness I cannot find elsewhere. Sometimes I count my steps or breaths. Other times I study the sway of the leaves, the flow of the water or the shapes in the clouds. Fears and resentments gently ebb away. When I'm walking in nature, everything is OK.

For swans, however, walking is an arduous unwelcome task. One of the mutes struggled across the snow-peppered ice to join its companions in the dark freezing-cold water. After three minutes I reached the five swans, poised like ornaments, the centrepiece of a classic English winter scene.

The word 'bird' does not suffice for this creature, but how could any such word do it justice? No end of scientific studies nor interrogations of myths will ever come up with any fact or insight that expresses the true magnificence of the swan. Nor will poetry, art or indeed a book ever quite capture its true beauty. For that remains its most prized attribute – swans are simply beautiful to watch. And that's what I did, for half an hour, mesmerised and enchanted as they floated silently, penned within the crusty edges of the lake as they paddled around the still liquid centre. Even their wake was elegant – two gentle lines diverged from the tail in a true V, trailing away from their bodies into the calm navy water.

Their demeanour was sombre, belying their anguished search for food. They were struggling in this bitter spell, and had probably spent the last few days scouring the local area for thawed ice and the weeds below.

But the scant food they found was merely paying for the journey. So here they were, oscillating once again between fragility and strength. Only moments earlier they had been sending mallard and pochard ducks scurrying for cover, their awesome power too much for most. But now I was closer. I could see their frames were slight, teetering on the edge of being in the depth of such a difficult winter. Their heads dipped below the surface, their rumps pointed at the harsh white skies. But they emerged with nothing. Their dangerously thin necks could not reach the vegetation in the warmer centre of the lake, which was far too deep; but its shallow fringes, where they would normally have fed, were far too frozen.

The bushes behind me began to rustle. Snow, fine as dust, sprinkled down from a small ragged bramble bush which engulfed a rotten picket fence. An old man emerged from the foliage, covered in powder snow. He held down the fence with one hand and used his body to push back the scratchy branches to form a gap. Through the opening his two grandchildren emerged.

'They've flown in every day – poor buggers.' The man was around 75 years old, bearded, enormous in height, breadth and character – fingers like chunky parsnips, no gloves. From each of his enormous pockets he pulled a cabbage – one of the best foods to give to swans. From his right boot, a pocket knife.

He began cutting off huge chunks of cabbage, handing them to his two granddaughters and also to me. We launched it as far across the lake as our chilly limbs and thick winter jackets would allow. One by one the majestic creatures flapped their enormous wings and launched themselves out of the bleak frosty water onto the dusty ice.

This time there was nothing comical about their walk, nothing oafish in their demeanour. This was survival. At first they prodded at the leaves, eager but suspicious. They then devoured at speed. The two cabbages were gone within minutes. Two medium-sized vegetables were not enough to satisfy five hungry swans.

'Better get yours out then, girls,' he said, smiling. They took off their brand-new Christmas rucksacks and opened them wide to reveal four more.

We stood in silence, the girls tossing the leaves, the great creatures edging closer still. The old man found a rugged wooden stump nearby, the remnant of a bench which had rotted away. He held aloft the bench's leg and hammered it down onto the ice in small gentle arcs. The swans made their way to the lake's broken edge and at last began feeding on the fresh weeds beneath. A small deed, but one which might have given these birds a chance of making it through the winter. An act of kindness from a stranger and so rewarding – not only for the swans.

TIMELINE

30 million BCE (circa)
Swans evolve from the
theropod dinosaur family
and begin roaming Europe.

900,000 BCE (circa)
Homo antecessor arrives in
Britain and begins hunting
swans with wooden sticks.

8,000–3,000 BCE
Hunting weapons become
more sophisticated – bows,
arrows and copper.

500 BCE
Swans begin to take on a
revered and 'mythic' status.

55 BCE
Romans arrive in Britain.
The hunting of swans
escalates.

84 CE
Plato's dialogue *Phaedo*
includes a passage from
Socrates suggesting that
swans sing before they die.

1191
Richard I (Lionheart)
returns from the conquest
of Cyprus with mute swans
to decorate the River
Thames.

1482
King Edward IV's Act for
Swans declares that all
swans belong either to
the crown or to wealthy
landowners.

1496
King Henry VII Act protects the eggs of swans. **1530** Michelangelo paints a version of the Greek myth *Leda and the Swan*.

1697
Black swan first discovered by Europeans in Australia.

1824
Society for the Prevention of Cruelty to Animals (RSPCA) is created.

1827–35
Hans Christian Andersen writes *The Ugly Duckling*.

1875–76
Tchaikovsky composes *Swan Lake*.

1889
Royal Society for the Protection of Birds (RSPB) is created.

1916
W. B. Yeats writes poem 'The Wild Swans at Coole'.

1923
W. B. Yeats writes poem 'Leda and the Swan'.

1950s
Series of raids by protesters on British 'fur farms' sees American mink released into the wild, causing chaos for native wildlife.

1956
Oil barge sinks in the River Thames at Battersea. The spill kills 243 mute swans.

1962
17 people die when a passenger plane flying from New York to Washington DC hits swans and crashes.

1962–63
The Big Freeze hits Great Britain. The cold and snow kills thousands of birds and animals.

1965
Wildfowl Trust study finds pylons and overhead cables are killing hundreds of young mute swans every year.

1971
Wild Creatures and Forest Laws Act means certain rights of the crown to wild animals are abolished. But the new law excludes swans, which remain the property of the Queen in most cases.

1976
Concorde, the swan of the aviation world, takes to the skies for its first commercial flight.

1979
Government begins process of outlawing toxic lead weights used by fishermen in rivers and lakes.

1980s/1990s
Huge breakthroughs in DNA sequencing suggest the swan evolved from dinosaurs earlier than other British birds.

1981
Wildlife and Countryside Act introduced, giving swans an extra layer of protection under conservation law.

2003
British Airways and Air France withdraw Concorde from service.

2012
Leveson Inquiry report dispels myth that eastern European immigrants are killing and eating numerous swans in England.

2012
Man is attacked by a swan in Chicago and drowns.

2015
Mute swan voted UK's seventh-favourite bird in a nationwide poll (which the robin wins).

ESSENTIAL SWAN
FACTS AND STATS

- Swans have their own star constellation: Cygnus (Latin for swan).

- Swans have been swimming on Earth's waters, flying in its skies and dawdling across its varied landscapes for 30 million years – far longer than humankind's six million.

- The mute swan is the first bird in modern-day UK bird books. Traditionally, field guides present species in taxonomic order, with those which evolved from dinosaurs earliest at the front of the book.

- The swan is thought to have broken away from the suspected common ancestor of all birds – the theropod dinosaur – before the other British birds.

- There are around 500,000 mute swans in the world.

- Swans are one of the few birds which can recognise individual human beings.

- While an average wild swan's lifespan is 12 years, some have lived up to 33 years in captivity when cared for with a nutritious diet.

- The average swan has around 25,000 feathers.

- Antarctica is the only continent on earth without swans.

- The fear of swans is known as kiknophobia or cygnophobia.

- Swans must eat a quarter of their own body weight every day to maintain a body temperature of 40.5 °C – that's around 3 kg (6.5 lbs) of weeds.

- The divorce rate among swans is around 15 per cent.

- Measurements:

  Length: 140–160 cm (55–63 in.)

  Wingspan: 208–238 cm (82–94 in.)

  Weight:10–12 kg (22–26 lb 7 oz.)

- Population:

  UK breeding: 6,400 pairs

  UK wintering: 74,000 birds

- Target body temperature: 40.5 °C (104.9 °F)

- Diet: Water weeds, insects, snails

- Average batch size: five or six eggs

- Egg size: 11 cm (4 in.) in length, 7 cm (3 in.) wide

- Egg weight: 340 g (12 oz.)

- Egg weight in proportion to body: 3.8 per cent

- Nest size: Two metres (6 ft 6 in.) wide / 30–60 cm (1–2 ft) tall

- Egg incubation period: 35–42 days
- Average number of surviving cygnets from egg clutch: Two
- Top flying speed: 60 mph

- Predators:

Foxes
Crows
Magpies
Jays
Ravens
Jackdaws
Squirrels
Badgers
Owls
Gulls
Herons
Snakes
Mink
Pike

WANT TO KNOW MORE ABOUT SWANS?

Dan Keel: I Like Bird
Dan's website features a range of bird and wildlife photographs including many of the images featured in this book.
Visit www.ilikebird.uk

Where to watch swans:

Abbotsbury Swannery
This site claims to be the only one on the planet in which people can roam through an actual colony of nesting mute swans.
Website: www.abbotsbury-tourism.co.uk/swannery
Address: New Barn Road, Abbotsbury, nr Weymouth, Dorset, DT3 4JG
Phone: 01305 871858
Email: info@abbotsbury-tourism.co.uk
Twitter: @DorsetSwannery
Facebook: @AbbotsburySwannery
Instagram: @abbotsburyswannery

Thatcham Nature Discovery Centre
The discovery centre features interactive wildlife displays. The surrounding site features a network of footpaths, meaning there is something for everyone, from short walks to longer hikes. The area is great for wildlife all year round.
Website: www.bbowt.org.uk

Email: ndc@bbowt.org.uk
Address: Lower Way, Thatcham, Berkshire, RG19 3FU
Twitter: @BBOWT_NatureDC

WWT Slimbridge

This wildlife reserve is 800 hectares (2,000 acres) in size, with a vast array of different habitats for birds and other wildlife. While it specialises in waterfowl, it receives many migrant visiting birds which arrive to breed or to escape colder northern weather during the winter.

Address: WWT Slimbridge, Bowditch, Slimbridge, Gloucestershire, GL2 7BT
Website: www.wwt.org.uk/wetland-centres/slimbridge
Phone: 01453 891900
Email: info.slimbridge@wwt.org.uk
Twitter: @WWTworldwide
Facebook: @WWTworldwide
Instagram: wwtworldwide

Richmond Park

This site is one of London's eight royal parks. It covers an area of 2,500 acres and is designated as a European Special Area of Conservation and Site of Special Scientific Interest. It supports a range of species of birds, insects, bats and wildflowers.

Website: www.royalparks.org.uk/parks/richmond-park
Address: Richmond Park Office, Holly Lodge, Richmond Park, Surrey, TW10 5HS
Phone: 0300 061 2200
Email: richmond@royalparks.org.uk
Twitter: @theroyalparks
Facebook: @RichmondParkLondon
Instagram: @theroyalparks

Rainham Marshes RSPB Reserve

This Essex site is part of the Thames Estuary and is easily accessible from central London. A huge array of wildlife can be found here including birds, dragonflies and water voles.

Website: www.rspb.org.uk

Address: New Tank Hill Rd, Purfleet, South Ockendon RM19 1SZ

Phone: 01708 899840

Email: rainham.marshes@rspb.org.uk

Twitter: @RSPBRainham

Facebook: @RSPBRainham

Bishop's Palace

This site is famous for the swans on the moat which ring a bell at the gatehouse for food. The tradition is believed to have started in the 1870s when the daughter of the then-bishop first taught the swans how to tug on the bell ropes. In 2019 the palace welcomed a new swan pair to the moat, thanks to Swan Rescue South Wales.

Website: www.bishopspalace.org.uk

Address: The Bishop's Palace, Wells, Somerset, BA5 2PD

Phone: 01749 988111

Email: info@bishopspalace.org.uk

Twitter: @Bishops_Palace

Facebook: @Bishopspalace

Instagram: @bishopspalacewells

London Wetland Centre

This 100-acre site is run by the Wildfowl & Wetlands Trust (WWT) and brings the countryside to the heart of the capital. Most years see 180 different species of bird spotted, including bitterns, peregrine falcons and a wide array of ducks. Frogs, lizards and water voles are often seen as well. There are six hides hidden among a maze of meandering footpaths.

Address: WWT London, Queen Elizabeth Walk, Barnes, London, SW13 9WT
Website: www.wwt.org.uk/wetland-centres/london/
Email: info.london@wwt.org.uk
Phone: 020 8409 4400
Twitter: @WWTLondon
Faceboook: @wwtlondon
Instagram: @wwtlondon

Swan rescues:

Swan Support

This rehabilitation centre rescues and treats injured and sick swans in the Thames Valley area. The charity works to educate the public about the effects humans can have on swans and other water birds.
Website: www.swansupport.org.uk
Address: Swan Support, Queen Mother Reservoir, Horton Rd, Datchet, Slough SL3 9HN
Phone: 01628 876336 / 07968 868172
Email: info@swansupport.org.uk
Twitter: @swan_support
Facebook: @SwanSupportCharity
Instagram: @swan_support

The Swan Sanctuary

This charity is on alert 24 hours a day and 365 days a year. It responds to calls from the public and dispatches local rescue squads to the scene in minutes. Rescuers are trained to provide 'frontline' emergency treatment while more seriously injured birds are taken to the sanctuary for intensive care. The facility features an x-ray room, an operating theatre and specialist equipment for treating swans injured by oil spills.

Suspicious or violent behaviour towards swans should be reported immediately to the police. But there are also people who can help if you ever see a swan injured or in distress. Call the Swan Sanctuary on 01932 240790 or Swan Support on 01628 876336.

Remember that moving, damaging or destroying a swan's nest is illegal, regardless of its location. If you ever see a nest looking vulnerable to damage by humans – such as on a footpath or near a road – you should call your local council and ask them to protect it with fencing.

If, however, it merely looks vulnerable to the natural elements – maybe flooding or high winds – leave it be. It may all turn out for the best. If it doesn't, the pair will learn for next time. And there will be a next time – because, as we know, swans usually live a long life, stay together and breed until they die.

Website: www.theswansanctuary.org.uk

Address: The Swan Sanctuary, Felix Lane, Shepperton, Middlesex, TW17 8NN

Phone: 01932 240790

Twitter: @Swan_Sanctuary

Facebook: @TheSwanSanctuaryuk

Instagram: @theswansanctuary

International Bird Rescue
Website: www.birdrescue.org

Nature and mental health:

Mind
Website: www.mind.org.uk/information-support/tips-for-everyday-living/nature-and-mental-health

Phone: 0300 123 3393

Email: info@mind.org.uk

Mental Health Foundation (Thriving with Nature guide)
Website: www.mentalhealth.org.uk/campaigns/thriving-with-nature/guide
Phone: 020 7803 1100
Email: supporter@mentalhealth.org.uk

Other information

Nature photography tips
www.expertphotography.com/nature-photography-tips

Radio 4 Tweet of the Day – The Mute Swan
www.bbc.co.uk/programmes/b03k5bnl

Swan Upping
www.royal.uk/swan-upping-2021

LIST OF ILLUSTRATIONS

1. A swan on the Duke of Northumberland River, London (Dan Keel, www.ilikebird.uk)
2. The classic image of two adoring swans. Home Park, London (Sue Lindenberg)
3. These three cygnets hatched within a few minutes of one another (Dan Keel, www.ilikebird.uk)
4. An exposed swan's nest at RSPB Strumpshaw Fen, Norfolk (Dan Keel, www.ilikebird.uk)
5. This cygnet went for its first swim just hours after birth (Dan Keel, www.ilikebird.uk)
6. Cygnets often hop onto the back of the pen when they are tired (Sue Lindenberg)
7. An adult mute swan splashes down in Home Park, London (Sue Lindenberg)
8. Swans at Bishop's Palace in Wells ring the bell every day for food. Former operations manager George Le Roy looks on (The Bishop's Palace)
9. A swan's legs are designed for swimming, not walking (Dr Ellie Rad)
10. A cob rises up from the water after chasing away a goose (Dan Keel, www.ilikebird.uk)

11. A frosty touchdown in Bushy Park, London (Sue Lindenberg)

12. A cob chases two Egyptian geese in Richmond Park, London (Dan Keel, www.ilikebird.uk)

13. Swans sometimes hoick up a leg to regulate body temperature (Dan Keel, www.ilikebird.uk)

14. Swan-snapping at Moor Green Lakes, Wokingham, Berkshire (Matt Keel)

15. The insides of a swan's bill are serrated to help tear plants from the riverbed (Dan Keel, www.ilikebird.uk)

16. A male mute swan in Adam's Pond, Richmond Park, London (Dan Keel, www.ilikebird.uk)

17. A swan comes in to land at Home Park, London (Sue Lindenberg)

18. A calm dawn scene in London's Bushy Park (Sue Lindenberg)

ABOUT THE AUTHOR

Photo © Matt Keel

Dan Keel is a lifelong birdwatcher who has been photographing wildlife for over a decade. He has written for the *Guardian, Daily Mail, EnviroNews* and *Birdwatching Magazine* in a 10-year journalism career which culminated in him editing an award-winning website and six regional newspapers across London and Kent. He moved to the Home Office as a media officer and then to the Commonwealth as Head of Media Relations, where he worked on issues such as climate change mitigation and ocean conservation. Dan runs the website www. ilikebird.uk, organises bird 'walk and talks' and is often invited to speak about birds to children in primary schools. He is a qualified private pilot.

ACKNOWLEDGEMENTS

Many thanks to all those along the way who have helped with Project Swan. I'm forever grateful for the encouragement of my parents, Sherrie and Rob, my brother Matthew and brother-in-law Drew. A special thank you to my brother Michael and sister-in-law Rachel for giving me an emergency home in which to write the book, and for supplying me with gin, tonic, whisky and chocolate Freddos while doing it.

The beautiful photographs from Sue Lindenberg and Dr Ellie Rad helped bring the swan to life on these pages, while Professor Chris Perrins was always on hand to answer my awkward questions about the swan's anatomy. Thank you to Mark George for giving my first draft a good seeing to, and to Summersdale's Debbie Chapman for believing in me, the swan and the idea; not to mention project manager Robert Drew and copy-editor Julian Beecroft for all their work.

The charities Swan Support and the Swan Sanctuary do incredible work to protect and rescue swans, but they've also been enormously helpful throughout this process. Likewise, the Abbotsbury Swannery and Bishop's Palace have always been happy to engage with my annoying queries.

Finally, I would like to thank my Dad for gently coaxing me into birdwatching as a child, for being such a kind and gentle companion on our many walks, for sharing his soup and for, well, being a great Dad.

NOTES

For a full list of references, please see www.ilikebird.uk/swanbook

Chapter One – The Mute Swan

1. Barnes, Simon 'Nature: the remarkable grace of the mute swan', *The Times*, 19 November 2017
2. Young, Peter *Swan* (2008, Reaktion Books), p.10
3. Wilmore, Sylvia Bruce *Swans of the World* (1974, Taplinger), p.26
4. Witherby, Jourdain, Ticehurst, Tucker *The Handbook of British Birds Volume III* (1943, Witherby), p.26
5. del Hoyo, Josep; Elliott, Andrew and Sargatal, Jordi *Handbook of the Birds of the World – Ostrich to Ducks* (1992, Lynx Edicions), pp.577–78
6. Snow, D. W. and Perrins, C. M. *The Birds of the Western Palearctic (Concise ed.)* (1998, Oxford University Press)

Chapter Two – The Lover

1. Young, Peter *Swan* (2008, Reaktion Books), p.16
2. Nicolson, Adam *The Seabird's Cry* (2018, William Collins), p.64
3. Cerny, Dr Walter *A Field Guide in Colour to Birds* (1975, Octopus Books Limited), p.298
4. Wilmore, Sylvia Bruce *Swans of the World* (1974, Taplinger), p.21
5. Young, *Swan*, p.16

Chapter Three – The Fighter

1. Wilmore, Sylvia Bruce *Swans of the World* (1974, Taplinger), p.42
2. Hutchison, Peter '"Hannibal" swan "kills 15 other birds"', *Daily Telegraph*, 17 September 2010
3. Young, Peter *Swan* (2008, Reaktion Books), p.19
4. Osborne, Samuel 'Swan kills dog in park as screaming onlookers watch in horror', *The Independent*, 2 July 2019
5. Wilmore, *Swans of the World*, p.36
6. Young, *Swan*, p.127
7. ibid. p.132
8. Wilmore, *Swans of the World*, p.186
9. ibid. p.60
10. Mills, David 'Dangers of tall buildings', *Birdwatch* magazine, October 2015, p.38
11. Young, *Swan*, p.137
12. ibid. p.124
13. Wilmore, *Swans of the World*, p.63

Chapter Four – The Myth

1. D News *How Much Force Does It Take To Break A Bone?* [video], YouTube. Youtube.com/watch?app=desktop&v=5LSB4StMu5c, 20 October 2016
2. ibid.
3. Young, Peter *Swan* (2008, Reaktion Books), p.151
4. Wilmore, Sylvia Bruce *Swans of the World* (1974, Taplinger), p.53
5. Nelson, Tammy 'Are we meant to be monogamous? Why people cheat, and the appeal of open relationships', *The Independent,* 10 March 2015
6. Young, *Swan*, p.43
7. Fitter, R. S. R. *London's Natural History* (1945, Collins)

8.   Wilmore, *Swans of the World*, p.70

9.   Young, *Swan*, p.141

10.   National Archives, Currency Converter 1270–2017, nationalarchives.gov.uk/currency-converter

11.   Young, *Swan*, p.143

12.   ibid. p.142

13.   Smith, Eliza *The Compleat Housewife: Or, Accomplish'd Gentlewoman's Companion* (1739, J and J Pemberton)

14.   Murray, Ross *The Modern Householder: A Manual Of Domestic Economy In All Its Branches* (1872, Frederick Warne and Co)

15.   Food History Jottings *A Swan Supper on the Thames*, foodhistorjottings.blogspot.com/search?q=swans, 21 August 2013

16.   Wilmore, *Swans of the World*, p.187

Chapter Five – The Aviator

1.   Wilmore, Sylvia Bruce *Swans of the World* (1974, Taplinger), p.15

2.   Barnes, Simon 'Nature: the remarkable grace of the mute swan', *The Times*, 19 November 2017

3.   Anon. 'Trail blazers – If aircraft can copy the way geese fly, everyone will benefit', *The Economist,* 7 December 2019, p.82

4.   Baxter, Andy 'Flocks Away!', *Birdwatch* magazine, October 2015, pp.36–37

5.   Price, A. Lindsay *Swans of the World – In Nature, History, Myth & Art* (1994, Council Oak Publishing), p.40

SELECT BIBLIOGRAPHY

Armstrong, Sally *Vintage Champagne on the Edge of Space – The Supersonic World of a Concorde Stewardess* (2015, The History Press)

Baker, J. A. *The Peregrine* (1984, Penguin)

Barnes, Simon *How to Be a Bad Birdwatcher: To the Greater Glory of Life*, (2012, Short Books)

Baxter, Andy 'Flocks Away!', *Birdwatch* magazine, October 2015, pp.36–37

Beeton, Samuel Orchart *Beeton's Book of Birds* (1862, S. O. Beeton)

Buffon, Cuvier and Lacepede *A Natural History of the Globe, and of Man; Beasts, Birds, Fishes, Reptiles and Insects – Volume III* (1831, C. Whittingham)

Carrington, Damian; Duncan, Pamela and Barkham, Patrick 'Watchdog permits 170,000 wild bird killings in five years', *The Guardian*, 22 February 2019

Cornell Lab 'What Is Taxonomic Order And Why Is It Used For The Sequence Of Birds In My Field Guide?', allaboutbirds. org/news/what-is-taxonomic-order-and-why-is-it-used-for-the-sequence-of-birds-in-my-field-guide, 16 November 2015

Fitter, R. S. R. *London's Natural History* (1945, Collins)

Hardman, Isabel *The Natural Health Service: How Nature Can Mend Your Mind* (2021, Atlantic Books)

Hickley, Matthew 'Sorry, poached swan's off: Calls for clampdown on river bandits from eastern Europe', *Mail Online*, 7 August 2007

Humble, Kate and McGill, Martin *Watching Waterbirds with Kate Humble & Martin McGill* (2011, Bloomsbury)

McGrath, Sheena 'We are Star Stuff – A blog about mythology – Apollo: The swan god', earthandstarryheaven. com/2015/04/22/apollo-swan

Merriam-Webster 'A Drudge of Lexicographers Presents: Collective Nouns – What do you call a group of cats? Dogs? Marmosets? Lawyers?', merriam-webster.com/words-at-play/a-drudge-of-lexicographers-presents-collective-nouns

Moss, Stephen *The Robin: A Biography* (2017, Square Peg)

Nicolaides, Mark 'Incubating Eggs', swanlife.com/incubating-eggs, 2020

PetMD Editorial 'Bird Flu in Birds', petmd.com/bird/conditions/respiratory/c_bd_Avian_Influenza, 27 June 2008

Price, A. Lindsay *Swans of the World – In Nature, History, Myth & Art* (1994, Council Oak Publishing)

Riley 'What Do Swans Eat? (7 Foods To Feed These Beautiful Birds)', natureinflight.com/what-do-swans-eat, 6 October 2018

Snow, D. W. and Perrins, C. M. *The Birds of the Western Palearctic (Concise ed.)* (1998, Oxford University Press)

The Royal Windsor website 'Swan Upping', thamesweb.co.uk/swans/upping2.html

The Swan Sanctuary 'Frequently Asked Questions – Swan related questions', theswansanctuary.org.uk/general-information

Wilmore, Sylvia Bruce *Swans of the World* (1974, Taplinger)

Yeats, William Butler *The Collected Works of W. B. Yeats* (1989, Macmillan)

Yeats, William Butler *The Collected Poems of W. B. Yeats* (1989, Collier Books)

Young, Peter *Swan* (2008, Reaktion Books)

INDEX

A

Abbotsbury, Dorset 60, 150, 237, 245

Andersen, Hans Christian 131, 232

Aphrodite 51

Apollo 51, 126

art 52–56, 125, 180, 228

aviation 175–184, 233

B

Baker, J. A. 30, 104, 249

ballet 14, 125, 128, 130, 131

Beeton, Samuel Orchart 69, 102, 249

Berkshire 26, 27, 100, 103, 118, 144, 187, 227, 238, 243

Bewick's swan 7, 8, 17, 18, 19, 40, 134, 185

bill/beak 8, 10, 11, 17, 18, 19, 35, 41–47, 52, 58–67, 70, 74–81, 92, 106, 111, 136– 145, 166, 196, 209, 213, 243

black swan 40, 134, 232

black–necked swan 40

bread 36, 69, 72, 83, 96, 152, 154, 159, 167, 168, 208

British Trust for Ornithology (BTO) 90, 99, 144, 222

Buffon, Georges–Louis Leclerc Comte de 14, 37, 48, 249

C

Concorde 175, 176, 184, 186, 233, 249

Coronavirus COVID–19 24, 119, 179, 218

coscoroba swan 41–43

courting 7, 63, 64, 139

cygnets 42, 57, 59, 66, 74–82, 91–95, 111, 119, 149–157, 168, 176, 184, 207, 236, 242

D

Denmark 45, 185

Department for Environment, Food and Rural Affairs (DEFRA) 120
Dyers' Company 141, 143, 144, 147, 161
diet 27, 44, 46, 167, 189, 234
dinosaurs 38, 39, 43, 48, 231, 233, 234
disease 144, 150, 220
DNA 39, 42, 233
dogs 14, 17, 72, 74, 94, 97, 137, 159, 168, 217

E
eggs 43, 52, 63–75, 82, 91–95, 107, 118–121, 131, 142, 185, 205, 231, 235, 236

F
feathers 12, 13, 17, 35, 36, 38, 43, 48, 57, 60, 64–80, 98–108, 116, 125, 137, 144, 167, 177, 184, 190, 203, 209–211, 234
feeding 47, 57–60, 66, 74–83, 106–109, 159, 165, 166, 168, 186, 205–209, 222, 230
fishermen 44, 99, 111, 112, 233
flight 13, 14, 17, 25–36, 46–48, 78–80, 98, 134–137, 168, 173–189, 210, 233

G
geese, Canada 79, 181, 195
geese, Egyptian 70–71, 208, 243
geese, greylag 14, 73, 97, 121, 187, 199, 208
Greece/Greeks 14, 43, 51, 54, 89, 96, 125, 126, 132–135, 173, 186, 232

H
habitat 18, 46, 96, 106, 183, 184, 187, 217–223
hunting/hunters 18, 90, 95–103, 117, 131, 135, 141, 150, 158, 217

I
Ireland 45

K
King Edward I 87
King Edward IV 97, 140, 145–147, 221, 231
King Henry III 151
King Henry VII 142, 231
King Richard I 97, 150–151, 231

L
lead 111–112, 117, 233
Leda 51–53, 125–126, 232
Leveson, Lord 162–163, 233
Lindo, David 19

London Wetland Centre 187–191

M

mating 7, 22, 56–68, 91, 93, 106, 148–149, 184

Michelangelo 53, 173, 232

migration 105, 108, 110, 184–185

moulting 47, 48, 96, 115, 144, 184–185

Murray, Ross 155

music 56, 102, 126, 133–136, 145, 146

myth 51–56, 89, 96, 125–169, 228, 231–233

N

Natural England 120–121, 223

neck 13, 30, 35, 43–48, 51, 56, 58–72, 83, 87, 91–93, 104–107, 153, 175, 191, 195, 196, 199, 208, 229

nest 21, 22, 57–82, 94, 102, 109, 117, 118, 120, 142, 148, 183, 184, 187, 189, 205, 217, 221, 235

Nicolson, Adam 58, 220

O

oil 52–53, 76, 112–117

P

paintings 17, 51, 53, 56, 87, 173

parenthood 67, 75–83, 94

Perrins, Professor Chris 41–42, 245, 246, 250

pets 14, 17, 72, 74, 94, 97, 137, 159, 168, 217

photography 7, 8, 38, 56, 59, 72, 76, 81, 147, 196, 198, 202–214, 241

Plato 51, 133, 200, 231

poetry 14, 51, 52, 54, 81, 101, 133, 156, 173, 175, 228, 232, 250

Poland 41, 45

Popham Airfield 33

predators 7, 12, 28, 44, 60, 63, 66, 76, 78, 87, 89, 90, 100, 105, 116, 168, 177, 184, 205, 217, 236

Price, A. Lindsay 248, 250

puffin 19, 20, 58, 115, 148, 160

pylons 28, 44, 100–107, 217, 232

Q

Queen Elizabeth I 98

Queen Elizabeth II 142

R

recipes 152–158

Richmond Park 67, 72, 81, 119, 208, 238, 243
robin 8–12, 19–22, 29, 65, 76, 121, 202, 233, 250
Romans 52, 87, 89, 97, 133, 173, 231
RSPB 45, 46, 106, 109, 146, 197, 217, 222, 232, 239, 242
RSPCA 120, 166, 222
Russia 18, 45, 125, 128, 219

S
Shakespeare, William 51, 88, 133, 148
Slimbridge Wetland Centre 18, 238
Swan Lake 51, 125, 128–131, 232
Swan Sanctuary, The 119, 166, 240, 245, 250
swan song 133, 134

T
Tchaikovsky 128, 131, 232
Thames, River 97, 98, 115, 143, 147, 150, 187, 189, 223, 231, 232, 239
Thatcham 31–32, 62–63, 118, 187, 202, 227, 237, 238
trumpeter swan 40, 134
tundra swan 18, 40
twitchers 26–27, 109, 187

U
Ugly Duckling 51, 125, 131–132, 232
upping 144, 241, 250

V
vandals 96, 117–120, 165, 217
Vintners' Company 141, 143, 144, 147, 157, 161, 176

W
whistling swan 18, 40, 134, 182, 189
whooper swan 7, 8, 17–19, 23, 40, 43, 44, 135, 145, 146, 185
windfarms 108–110
wings 11–14, 26, 30, 35, 52, 55–56, 64, 71–78, 92–95, 101, 105, 111, 134, 136–140, 158, 167, 173–191, 208–212, 230
Wildfowl & Wetlands Trust (WWT) 99, 100, 106, 168, 187, 232
Yeats, W. B. 52, 173, 232, 250

Y
Young, Peter 89, 246–250

Z
Zahavi, Amotz 58
Zeus 51–52, 126

Have you enjoyed this book?
If so, why not write a review on your favourite website?

If you're interested in finding out more about our books,
find us on Facebook at **Summersdale Publishers**,
on Twitter at **@Summersdale** and on Instagram at
@summersdalebooks and get in touch. We'd love
to hear from you!

Thanks very much for buying this Summersdale book.

www.summersdale.com